C0-AQW-198

Creating
Balance *in Your*
Child's Life

Beth Wilson Saavedra
Author of *Meditations for New Mothers*

CB
CONTEMPORARY BOOKS

Library of Congress Cataloging-in-Publication Data

Wilson, Beth (Beth Shannon)
    Creating balance in your child's life / Beth Wilson Saavedra.
       p.   cm.
    ISBN 0-8092-2875-0
    1. Child rearing.   2. Parenting.   3. Stress in children.   4. Time
pressure.   I. Title.
    HQ767.9.W54   1999
    649'.1—dc21   99-26800
                                                  CIP

Cover and interior design by Mary Lockwood
Cover illustration copyright © 1999 EyeWire, Inc.

Published by Contemporary Books
A division of NTC/Contemporary Publishing Group, Inc.
4255 West Touhy Avenue, Lincolnwood (Chicago), Illinois 60712-1975 U.S.A.
Copyright © 2000 by Beth Wilson
All rights reserved. No part of this book may be reproduced, stored in a retrieval
system, or transmitted in any form or by any means, electronic, mechanical,
photocopying, recording, or otherwise, without the prior written permission of
NTC/Contemporary Publishing Group, Inc.
Printed in the United States of America
International Standard Book Number: 0-8092-2875-0
99 00 01 02 03 04 MV 19 18 17 16 15 14 13 12 11 10 9 8 7 6 5 4 3 2 1

To my son, Alexander, who is an inspiration and a profound teacher, I love you with all my heart.

Here is my wish for you. May we all, parents and children alike, live from the rich fullness of who we are. In the eloquent and insightful words of Audre Lorde:

> *I find I am constantly being encouraged to pluck out some one aspect of myself and present it as a meaningful whole, eclipsing or denying the other parts of self. But this is a destructive and fragmenting way to live. My fullest concentration of energy is available to me when I integrate all the parts of who I am, opening, allowing power from particular sources of my being to flow back and forth freely without restrictions of externally imposed definitions.*

> —FROM "HOLISTIC POLITICS:
> DIFFERENCE IS OUR STRENGTH,"
> *Ms. Magazine*

Contents

ACKNOWLEDGMENTS   VII

INTRODUCTION   IX

1 Why Balance Matters   1

2 Is Your Child out of Balance?   11

3 Your Child's Unique Temperament   39

4 Meaningful Activities Worth Making Time For   55

5 Creating Balance in the Electronic Age   77

6 Nourishing with Nature   89

7 The Importance of Healthy Living   99

8 Mentors and Guides   121

9 Building Character and Optimism   131

10 Communication and Balance   151

11 Humor as a Way to Create Balance   165

APPENDIX 1   The Myers-Briggs Personality Types   173

APPENDIX 2   Other Systems for Understanding
              Temperament   217

INDEX   249

Acknowledgments

I have many people to thank and many people to be thankful for . . .

To my parents, Anne, Paul, and Linda, I thank you for giving me the gift of life and wide eyes with which to view the world and her people.

To my grandparents, I hold all of you in my heart, always.

To Jon, Sara, and Matthew. I hold a special place for each one of you in my heart. With deep gratitude and abundant love.

To my dear, dear friends, who are such incredible and exceptional people, I love you: Rose Benstock, Maris Allen, Linda D'Agrosa, Nancy Edison, Betsy Allen, Ginger Hinchman-Birkeland, Caroline Douglas, Daryn Stier, Marie Hartley, Laura Gill and Ella, Christine Ciavarella, Jeanine Martin, Kelsey Brendel, Uma/Trish Schaef, Lee Smith, Sally Smith, Eric Lieberman, Todd Nelson, Brad Pearsall, Nathan Josephs, Lee Cook, Jessica Donnelly, Nancy Ison, Deirdre Mueller, Cindy Olsen, Kenny, Nikki, Jackie, and Nicole Arends, and Morgan Soderberg.

A special thank you to Jillian Klarl for mothering me in a way nobody else could.

To the George family—Joann, Mario, Dave, Vera, John, Cindy, Rob, and Diane—I extend a warm embrace of thanks for welcoming us into your family.

My editor, Judith McCarthy, has been incredibly helpful in bringing this book to life. A big thank you! I look forward to working with you again. To Kara Leverte, who helped me to conceive the idea for this book, thank you. And big-time thanks to Susan Moore-Kruse, senior project editor, for all her hard work.

I have the privilege of working with a bright, warm, and supportive agent, Nancy Crossman. Many thanks for believing in me and my work.

Introduction

We live in a complex world. Our lives are busy, usually too busy. As parents, we have the job of juggling our own schedules with the added responsibility of helping our children to structure their time. We arrange child-care programs; we call the local community centers to find classes of interest; we sign our children up for team sports, play groups, ballet lessons, and computer courses. Not only do we create ways for our children to pursue their talents, interests, and passions, but we must also take care to assist them with the more concrete aspects of becoming capable, conscientious individuals who can successfully and resiliently navigate through the current state of affairs. Certainly, we want our children to flourish, yet we may worry that we are not properly equipping them for the future. In our attempt to "cover all bases," we may complicate our children's lives unnecessarily, forgetting to trust the cadence of their unique development and the importance of learning through joyful means such as playing and exploring or simply being in the presence of nature. As bestselling author Thomas Moore points out in his book *The Re-Enchantment of Everyday Life*, "A child's weekly schedule of lessons and 'experiences' can sometimes compete with that of a CEO of a large company. This kind of education appears to arise out of anxiety, the fear that the child may not be able to get along or 'compete.' "

It is often difficult for us, as parents, to keep our perspective. On the news, we hear about America's children falling behind other nations', we see advertisements encouraging us to enroll our toddlers in speed-reading programs, and we overhear conversations in the park where parents are charting their children's academic milestones as closely as the numbers on Wall Street. It isn't surprising that we feel pressure to "encourage" our children to excel. During a recent conversation with Kara Leverte, an editor at NTC/Contemporary Publishing Group and a mother of three, we discussed how easily a mother can succumb to feelings of doubt. We find ourselves worrying and wondering: "Am I keeping up with my children's interests?" "Am I making sure they're on par with their peers?" "Am I involving my children in enough activities and giving them ample opportunity to excel?" "Am I structuring their time so it will be quality time, or are there more beneficial ways to meet my child's intellectual, emotional, and spiritual needs?" Yet, as we reflected on our own styles of parenting, we realized that we are given many chances to actively pursue an interest, teach a skill, or master a talent. In other words, if we occasionally missed an opportunity to offer our child a formalized structure for participating in an enjoyed activity, the opportunity was not lost forever. In fact many of us have learned from experience that our eagerness to encourage an activity can actually thwart movement toward developing love of a sport, an art activity, or musical talent.

It is helpful to remember that our children's growth can be more likened to cycles and spirals and stops and starts than a linear path that follows a logical sequence. And, although it is tempting to view our children's growth in linear terms, most of us have observed that it is anything but linear. Because a child's growth is like buds that blossom only to close and open again, it is not paramount that we push every subject our children show interest in, nor pursue every talent and natural ability with the same intensity.

Moreover, we live in a society that places a disproportionate value on busyness and actively keeping busy. Rarely do we hear about the necessity of reflection, savoring a moment, standing in reverence, absorbing a thought or concept deeply within the matrix of our minds, allowing the muse or natural tempo of life to arise, or insisting on solitude for inner peace and inspiration. For this reason, it is essential to teach our children about balance. Because, just as we must pull back from the centrifugal forces of today, so, too, must our children learn the value of steadying their minds, replenishing their spirits, resting their bodies, and tending to the inherent needs a child has for enjoying the more poetic side of life through imagination, play, magic, love, tenderness, and joy. Needs that can only be met through giving our children the unrushed time and space to simply *be*.

As all parents quickly learn, children possess their own temporal cadence, and rarely, if ever, are they in a hurry. For this reason, it is children who most often remind us of the importance of slowing down and absorbing the unique dimensions of a snowflake, the curious movement of a snail in the garden, and the brilliant reflections cast off a fine jewel or the ocean waves. As my close friend Jeanine Martin, a mother of three, told me, "My children demanded that I relax and be in the present moment—and it has made all the difference." And, recently, *Newsweek* mirrored this fact: "Science confirms what wise parents have long known: kids need lots of time and attention." Barbara DeAngelis, author of the *New York Times* bestseller *Real Moments*, puts it this way: "Paying attention to the moments in your life as they unfold is what having real moments means, moments when you are fully present, fully feeling, fully alive. Sometimes they will be moments of great happiness. Sometimes they will be moments of profound sorrow. But always, when you pay attention to where you are and what is going on, right now, you will experience a moment that has meaning, a moment that matters, and that is what I call a real moment." But why is "unrushed time" so important? Simply, because it keeps us in touch with the beauty and authenticity of our lives—and this feeds our souls and spirits. While listening to National Public Radio one day, I heard an interview with a famous Norwegian explorer. When asked how he was able to traverse the Arctic by himself with only a sparse amount of supplies carried on a sled, he responded like this: "Some mornings I would wake up and look at the endless stretches of snow and ice and feel the bitter cold of such a seemingly bleak landscape, and I would feel overwhelmed by my journey until I opened my eyes to the sparkling snow crystals, the vibrant color of the sky, the formations in the ice. I was inspired by the beauty and this urged me on, reminding me of the purpose of my trek."

Certainly, as parents, providing real moments within the rapid pace of our current lifestyles can be difficult and frustrating. How many times have we attempted to load our brood into the car to run errands or arrive at school on time only to be greeted by a scenario such as this: you run around the house making sure you have your belongings—purse, diaper bag, car keys, briefcase, coat, and lists. Then you go down the line asking each child if he or she has everything he or she needs: shoes tied, sweatshirt on, backpack with homework tucked inside, lunch box full, toys for the drive, and teeth brushed. All of you go out the door, remember you forgot something, then come back in the door. Walk down the front path. Walk back up it. Your toddler inspects every dead insect, flower bud, and piece of refuse along the way. He protests after being told for the fourth time to climb into the car because "we're running late." The older children fight over the front seat, and they all want to take part in scraping the ice off the windshield. Sound familiar? Although our children's interest in their surroundings, need for their own inner agendas, and tendency to move at a sloth's pace may aggravate and frustrate adults who are accustomed to jumping from one activity to the next, they provide us with an important lesson in being present to the moment (paying complete attention with all of our senses) and absorbing the richness of life. Although it is not always workable to take our time, it is important to be aware of creating more real time.

In a culture that has cultivated, and more recently pursued, a course of so-called realism whereby those things that fill and illuminate the spirit—charm, beauty, love, playfulness, innocence, serendipity, and genuine leisure—are viewed with a skeptical suspicion that can eclipse the sacredness of life with an overly stern practicality, it is essential that we, as parents, keep our perspective. Otherwise, the landscape of life looks bleak indeed. As Moore puts it,

> Some psychological theories equate childhood with paradise and conclude that to live as mature adults we should separate heroically from childhood and enter this vale of tears called maturity. They're afraid that if we don't overcome childhood, we'll become stuck in infantile illu-

sions. Some experts believe that life is fundamentally dis-enchanted and that those who think otherwise are naive and psychotic. During my years as a psychotherapist, I felt that people bringing me their stories of a foundering career, a failing marriage, a tenacious depression, or an overpowering addiction were suffering from a deeper malaise. They had fallen out of love with life itself, which, in their adult years, had become an absorbing col-lection of problems . . . On the other hand . . . I encounter many people who are able to avoid falling into easy modern despair, who love their lives and themselves, who have endured all kinds of suffering, from divorce to cancer, and yet express and cultivate their love of life in gardening, painting, travel, music and community ser-vice. Another secret for re-enchanting everyday life is to refuse to leave Eden, to be in the garden for life. If we imagine paradise deeply enough, we won't be literally childish or naive, but we can live with a positive love of life amid many kinds of torment.

But why don't we enter this domain with our children more frequently, especially when they always seem to know the myriad of entry points? Moore answers the question this way: "It seems we're afraid of paradise, anxious, perhaps, that the orderly world we know will fall apart if the angel guarding Eden's gates lowers his sword for a second of rest."

With this kind of anxious and unimaginative view of life, which is often reflected in warnings for parents to rush their children into the future as virtually masters of every-thing, it is not surprising that the rate of depression among children is rising at an alarming pace. Focusing solely on the need to equip our children for the future without including inspiration, optimism, and a love of life with all its complexities as tools they need for their proverbial tool belt is setting them up for possible material success but little else. It is our job, then, as parents, to bridge this gap. Not only for our children's sake, but for our own. Balance is the key.

In *Creating Balance in Your Child's Life*, I begin by discussing the importance of balance. Next, I have included information on the effects of stress because, like it or not, we live in a complex world that bombards us with information and assaults our senses daily. Both adults and children need to find effective and enjoyable ways to reduce negativity and tension because parental stress has a profound impact on children's anxiety, and our children often need assistance with developing positive methods for coping. Then I present helpful ways for identifying children's stress signals and bringing more balance into their lives by understanding individual temperaments because children are very different from one another—even within the same family. Understanding your child's individual needs can help you more readily identify which kinds of activities will help your child flourish and those that will drain or overwhelm a particular child, inadvertantly adding to his or her stress. In addition, I provide a section on health because many lifestyle changes can be made, including the reduction of stress, to improve our children's physical, mental, and emotional well-being.

You will also find a variety of information designed to encourage meaningful and rejuvenating activities that increase genuine quality time. This awareness can assist parents in creating new paradigms for lifestyles that nourish and support our families of today, helping them to grow instead of simply survive. Next, I focus on what, specifically, we can do for our children, not only to prepare them for the future, but to assist them in embracing the present. We will explore a variety of activities; ways to create sacred, unhurried time; character-building experiences; and resources for navigating the options available to children: everything from creative projects you can do at home to activities aptly suited to your child's needs. I will give suggestions for determining which of your child's passions and interests to pursue as well as methods for locating individuals in your community who can provide wisdom, enthusiasm, encouragement, and inspiration and help us to "set them on their path." Last, I have created a section of old-fashioned activities, simple things to do around the house, in a nearby park, or out in nature that can slow us down and strengthen the bonds we share. In fact, it will give you the opportunity to incorporate activities that you found special as a child into your daughter or son's life.

I hope this book will remind you of the wonderful parent you already are and assist you in becoming more of the parent you want to be. Use it as a tool to remember what you and those close to you can offer, to express the qualities of who you are, so you may be a living example as well as a guide for your children as they continue to discover and bring forth the unique potential they have inside.

Resources

The Re-Enchantment of Everyday Life, by Thomas Moore. New York: HarperCollins, 1997.
Newsweek, "Off to a Good Start: Why the First Three Years Are Crucial to a Child's Development," by Barbara Kantrowitz, Spring/Summer 1997 Special Edition: pp. 6–9.
Real Moments, by Barbara DeAngelis. New York: Dell Publishing, 1995.

1

Why Balance Matters

Recently, while visiting my parents in Boston for the holidays, I heard a newscaster report that the response of individuals polled as to what they wanted more than anything else was that they wanted more time. I suspect that if the reporter had extended the questionnaire to children, the response would have been similar.

Time certainly has become a scarce commodity. Yet, often, instead of relishing it, we attempt to cram as many things into it as we can. And when our lives become overcrowded and chronically rushed, so do our children's. We bounce them from school to ballet classes to sports activities to music lessons, then come home to complete reading lists and homework assignments. Every minute of every day is scheduled. Free time is practically a thing of the past.

Today it is all too easy to become enmeshed in the frantic pace of our society. After all, the pressure to keep up and excel is everywhere. The focus is not on cultivating our individual gifts at a soul level (gifts that are innate and indistinguishable from the individual's essence), but rather on developing skills and talents that can be applied to the corporate track. Don't misunderstand me—striving for excellence is a worthwhile goal. But doing so at the expense of a quality life is another story altogether. Think about it. What is success? How does our society determine success? Is a successful child a truly fulfilled child or one who bases his self-worth on material gain? A child who enjoys what he engages in, or a person who is anxious because he is trying to please others and live up to their expectations? A child who is given the opportunity to have a variety of fresh experiences he enjoys or a child who is forced to participate? Certainly, the majority of children must do things or try programs they may not like. Yet if we are to honor our children's individuality, we will respect their choices, we will respect their limits, respect their need for alone time, and respect their need to simply play and be children instead of miniature adults.

To enroll our children in too many activities at once in an attempt to "give them the best of everything" or to "try out everything they show interest in, just in case they are destined to be the next world champion" or to "make sure they are well prepared" is overwhelming—and it complicates our children's lives unnecessarily. Of course, we mean well. Yet, if we are not careful, the results can be harmful, and in some cases, disastrous. As Dr. David Elkind points out in his book *The Hurried Child: Growing Up Too Fast Too Soon*, "Parents are overprogramming their children." He says, "No longer do we see children as innocent and in need of protection . . . in the postmodern world we need to see children as competent. Instead of protecting children, our emphasis is on preparing them." A January 1997 article in *Bay Area Parent* reports that when asked why parents tend to have this view, Dr. Elkind responded, "Their competence to handle all these programs they are in is our adult need to have competent children. Because if we didn't believe our children could handle before-and-after school care, divorce, all the stuff they see on television, we'd probably go nuts as parents." Yet, as Dr. Elkind and many others can attest, the dangers of overscheduling are obvious and can be summed up in one word: *stress*. Children today are exhibiting a plethora of symptoms: sleeping problems, eating disorders, pulling hair, biting nails, having trouble focusing, feeling aggressive, feeling nervous exhaustion that translates into hyperactive behavior patterns, withdrawing, and developing fears and phobias, to name a few. It is up to us, then, as parents, to create balance in our children's lives by monitoring the number of classes and activities; making sure our children, including teenagers, get enough sleep; watching for signs of stress and taking action to decrease it; protecting our children from being exposed to more than they can handle; and cuddling and soothing our children when they need the assurance that tells them we love them no matter what.

Let's face it. As adults, we are abundantly capable of knowing when our children are out of sorts. And although we may not always be able to remedy the situation immediately, we can make changes that allow our young ones to feel more balanced and relaxed. As studies show, when parents reduce the number of their children's activities and allow their children to take the lead in making choices about experiences and classes they would like to participate in (or not), many of the stress signals disappear. In fact, in a November 1997 *New York Times* article, a therapist noted, "I had so many children in my office who barely had time to schedule appointments with me. As it turned out, when their parents didn't put so much pressure on them, and cut back on their activities, these children didn't need to see me regularly for their problems because the majority of their problems stemmed from too much stress." To quote one of my favorite bumper stickers, "For fast-acting relief, try slowing down." Not surprisingly, when we slow down, our children slow down, and we have the wonderful opportunity to connect with those we love. Instead of time being a scarce commodity to be doled out and used up, we can create time to move at the speed of life—not the speed of light.

The Importance of Unrushed Time

I learned an important lesson from my nine-year-old son, Alexander, about the importance of unrushed time. One morning we were zooming through the kitchen preparing for school, and I was feeling incredibly efficient as I threw his lunch together, gulped down breakfast, gathered my things, and headed for the door. I felt like a drill sergeant with a well-run team. Then, when Alexander and I got in the car, he started to cry. "Mommy, I *hate* to rush," he told me, tears streaming down his face. Instantly, I realized that I didn't like it any more than he did. And even though I knew better than to apply workaholic executive procedures to my family, I had fallen into the habit, feeling there was no other way to prepare for the day. But the fact is, there is another way to prepare for the day. The only requirement is that we be mindful to the moment. Now I make a point of taking five to ten minutes to snuggle with Alexander as he first opens his eyes. Then I leave him to change into clean clothes, brush his teeth, and gather his things. Next, we meet in the kitchen for a small breakfast, and I prepare his lunch (he gets to make some of the food choices according to his preferences). Sometimes we still have to pick up the pace toward the end, but overall, we have time to touch base in the morning, and we both feel better because of it. During the fifteen-minute ride in the car, we have a chance to talk, plan our weekend, discuss his homework or other topics being addressed at school, or simply be silent together, holding hands. I can guarantee that we both feel more relaxed. We begin our days with less tension and stress, and we take the time, if only fifteen minutes, to nurture our loving bond with each other. Certainly, each child is different, but for my three kids, touch of any kind—stroking, hugging, holding—is essential to their well-being. It balances out the fast-paced world they must contend with every day at school.

Another way of creating unrushed time is to leave days where the schedule is completely open and putter around the house. My mother is a professional putterer. She can clean closets, rearrange clothes, empty the freezer, organize her video collection, play the piano, and just do nothing for hours. The only other times I have seen her this relaxed are when she collects shells at the beach. Suspending time is meditative. It allows connections to be made, sacred spaces to open up without planning or manipulation. I remember resisting doing the dinner dishes until my stepmother, Linda, told me a story about how easy it was for her to talk with her mother while she washed and her mother dried. "There was something about joining together to do these ordinary chores that allowed us to open our hearts to each other and let our guard down, our differences slipped away, so we could speak words that were rarely spoken." From that day forward, I had a much greater appreciation for the simple rituals that shape our lives, creating a safe space to speak our minds and hearts.

Unrushed time allows us to be present to our children, to what they have to say, and they can feel our availability. Otherwise, if we only casually listen or are constantly preoccupied, they sense it. And, if this persists, our children can withdraw from us and feel as though we are not emotionally available to them—which we are not. For many children, this is a big source of anxiety. If our children cannot depend on us to be there emotionally for them, who do they turn to when they are confronted with difficult challenges? A bully at school who is making life miserable? A math problem that they consistently have trouble with, which makes them feel inadequate? Obviously, when we are perpetually rushed and our schedules are overflowing with obligations, we miss out on these spontaneous moments and the opportunities they bring to allow us to embrace those we love.

It is also important for our children to learn the value of unrushed time. Otherwise, they can become addicted to being busy. They easily become bored if they are not entertained, and, sadly, as many studies confirm, their attention span and ability to concentrate for any significant length of time is diminished. When this happens, many children seek out stimulation: long hours of TV viewing, constant playing of the radio, even sugary or caffeinated foods such as cookies, chocolate, and carbonated sodas to keep themselves running at a high pitch. Then, they crash. It is not difficult to see how this pattern can be disruptive to everyday functioning, especially if it becomes a vicious cycle. As parents, we must assist our children in learning ways to relax and "come down" naturally—and to learn that slow is not necessarily dull. When I was taking an improvisation class at Stanford, the motto was "Dare to Be Dull." I quickly learned what this meant. Instead of performing scenes that were designed to be clever, funny, or interesting, each student had to open to the moment of possibility and allow the scene to emerge from thin air instead of premeditated ideas of what would be great. Our instructor put it in these terms: "The first words and actions are a gift given to you from the person who begins the exercise. For you to ignore what is before you and come up with your own idea for how the scene should go is a rejection of the gift. For you to assume that you know what is the best for the scene instead of allowing the scene to show you is arrogant." I quickly discovered how true her words were. Only when I was present to the scene in the same way I am present to my writing could I surrender to the potential brilliance of the moment and respond accordingly. Otherwise, I would spend all my time and energy controlling the scene, trying to rush it along to be what I envisioned it should be. Children can get caught up in trying to be constantly in charge, constantly in motion, constantly anticipating the next activity; and, because we are human, and not machines, this very attitude, although sometimes subtle, can create incredible stress, especially if the outcome is not as one expected. Because our society places high value on maintaining control, setting goals, and meeting projections, the balance is in creating enough unrushed time that our children can come to flourish in the moment and value what they can create in that moment. To do that, we must be willing to simplify our children's lives, and possibly our own.

Certainly, classes and exposure to various experiences assist our children in developing social skills and finding areas of interest. But, taken all together, even too many fun things can add up to tension and stress. We would do well to ask ourselves why we are providing so many structured activities throughout the day, every day. Often, it is because of our own needs and expectations, not our children's. Or, possibly, we want to please our little ones and give them the best of everything. However, there is such a thing as overkill, and although our intentions are admirable, we may be inadvertently sending messages we are not anticipating. In a November 1997 *New York Times* article, Dr. Lawrence Kutner puts it this way: "While the parents' motives and goals are good, their children may see things in a different light. They long for an opportunity to structure their own time, to be able to sit quietly and daydream for a few hours. To these children, the constant barrage of activities may come across as more of a punishment than a gift." Under these circumstances, it is not difficult to see why children may interpret overscheduling as a punishment or a way for their parents to avoid them. The movie *The Truth About Cats & Dogs* illustrates this point in a humorous yet truthful way. A woman calls in to a radio station to speak with the vet who answers people's pet-problem questions on the air. The woman is distressed because her German shepherd keeps destroying her apartment whenever she goes out for any length of time. The vet reminds the caller that although she sees it as a personal slight against her, the dog is simply acting out his feelings about her absence. The vet says something to this effect: "It's not like your dog is ecstatic that you're leaving so he can spend time finishing his novel. He wants to be with you." By the same token, some children's response to overscheduling is, "My parents must not have time for me, and they don't value me enough to make time for me." As a result, they may act out or withdraw. Or they may become reticent about spending time away from home by turning down invitations to birthday parties, sleep overs, and outings with their friends. Dr. Alice Sterling Honig, of Syracuse University, had this to say in a 1997 *New York Times* article: "What they really want scheduled is time alone with their parents."

Stress Is Serious

As we all know, life can be stressful. For children, it is becoming more stressful. Not only is the world more complex, with tougher choices to make earlier on, but even positive stress can exacerbate any existing tensions children may have to contend with. (By positive stress I mean exciting, exhilerating events in children's lives that, although positive, can be stressful and cause fatigue. Soccer playoffs, swim meets, science contests, and so forth, can all create positive stress.) And, if our lives are out of balance, you can bet our children's will be. They feel our tension over financial issues, marital problems, excessive worries, and chronic anger. Fortunately, our children send warning signals early on, giving us a chance to be the loving parents we are and to respond to their distress. We can teach our children that stress is a part of life, but that it need not become a lifestyle because there are positive ways of dealing with it.

In the next chapter, we look at the telltale signs of stress and ways we, as parents, can assist our children before stress becomes chronic. We will also explore the more serious effects of stress—phobias, eating and anxiety disorders, and other imbalances—that can severely influence our children's success and fulfillment in life. Remember, one of the most important assets you have in reducing tension and creating balance is you. Elaborate plans of action may be necessary in some instances. Yet, for the most part, we can create a more harmonious life for our children *and* ourselves by making wise choices and realigning our priorities.

Resources

The Hurried Child: Growing Up Too Fast Too Soon, by Dr. David Elkind. Boulder, Colo.: Perseus Books, 1989.

Bay Area Parent, "Interview with Dr. David Elkind," January 1997, p. 27.

KidStress, by Georgia Witkin, Ph.D. New York: Penguin/Putnam, 1999.

New York Times, "Parent and Child," by Dr. Lawrence Kutner, November 1997.

The Truth About Cats and Dogs, directed by Michael Lehmann, 97 minutes, Twentieth Century Fox, 1996.

2

Is Your Child out of Balance?

Balance is important. We need time to rest and rejuvenate. To do nothing except think, or not think. We need time to switch our focus away from goals and be present to the moment. We need time to play, visit with friends, and relax with our family. We need time to listen and to be heard, to bake, or to ride our bikes just because we feel like it. Far too often we get caught up in doing, doing, doing and going, going, going, forgetting the simple pleasures that make life worth living. As my good friend Betsy Allen always says, "It's like we're trying to live our lives on fast-forward, always striving." The result is stress and tension, restless sleep, and a vague feeling that serenity is an illusion or just out of reach.

Adults are not the only ones feeling this way. Children are exhibiting stress and the symptoms associated with it. In an article on "Stress Reduction" in *Natural Way* magazine, Andrew Scrivani puts it this way: "Now, a diverse education is absolutely necessary to the development of a well-rounded child. But it comes at a price: Endless rounds of piano, ice skating, and swimming lessons, followed by afternoons devoted to Little League and evenings with Cub Scouts or Brownies, topped off by weekend classes in karate and art appreciation create a lack of their own time simply to experience childhood. A strictly regimented, grueling schedule takes something out of the child—the kid in him."

When we overschedule our children, we run the risk of obscuring their individual identities with an overabundance of activities, and the child can become lost. Instead of choosing activities that are well suited to our children's ages and their temperaments, we may, out of parental concern for their futures, attempt to shape them into images of who we think they should be, not who they are. Or, what we think corporations, universities, or government institutions want them to be. Instead of helping our children bring out their best, we can get caught up in the trap of overprogramming them for the future because we are certain that music lessons, computer classes, or science camp will look good on their résumés. Unfortunately, what often happens is that children grow up to be sophisticated adults who haven't a clue as to who they are. In addition, the future we so carefully shaped them for may be obsolete. Wouldn't it be better to follow our children's lead, finding out what their interests are before signing them up for a formalized class? Couldn't we better serve our children by allowing them to try out a variety of activities before committing to an extended involvement in one or two areas of interest? Perhaps simply asking them if they would like to participate in a gymnastics class or swimming or chess lessons would be a good start. If, however, you are the parent of a child who has many interests and cannot say no to any of them, you might want to try scaling back or rotating them throughout the year. Remember, even positive stress is stress, and it can create the same results: anxiety, sleep deprivation, stomachaches, headaches, crying bouts, chronic fatigue, a shortened attention span, nail biting, irritable disposition, constipation, and so on.

How Can I Tell if My Child Is Stressed?

Fortunately, most signs of stress are hard to miss because the symptoms are exhibited in a variety of ways. The most obvious are physical symptoms and changes in behavior.

Physical Symptoms: stomachaches; headaches; increased colds, infections, and allergies; diarrhea; constipation; panic attacks; insomnia; swallowing difficulties; cold sweats; memory loss; dizziness; chest pains; backaches and neck aches; complaints of generally not feeling well; chronic fatigue; and dramatic loss or increase of appetite.

The fact is, chronic stress greatly inhibits a child's immune system, making her more vulnerable to common colds, skin disorders, asthma and allergies, and infections and viruses, as well as digestive problems. In fact, hormones produced under stress can eventually repress the production of certain white blood cells that help promote good health and proper immune functioning. If the body does not have time to rest and replenish and it must constantly deal with unrelenting stress, it will send out distress signals such as those listed above.

Behavioral Changes: bedwetting; arguing with siblings; acting out; moodiness; regression (babylike behavior); anxiety attacks; withdrawing from social activities and friends; fighting; acts of aggression, including hurting animals; restlessness; excessive daydreaming; excessive whining and crying; refusing to go to school, to go over to a friend's house, or to participate in after-school care; being overly clingy; swearing; using put-downs and caustic humor; being bossy and overly controlling; teasing siblings relentlessly; pouting; blaming others instead of taking responsibility for his own actions; biting nails; and trying to use humor and clever quips to avoid listening to others and taking them seriously.

If you suspect that your child is overextended, consider asking yourself the following questions:

- Does your child show little interest in new things?
- Is he cranky and tired most of the time?
- Is she withdrawn and somber?
- Is he moody? Does he cry easily over the slightest cause?
- Has she lost interest in activities that used to be important to her?
- Is most of his time scheduled, making spontaneous activities almost impossible?
- Does she have to stay up late to finish homework?
- As a parent, are you always aware of the time, thinking about where you need to be next?
- Do you spend the majority of your time chauffering and scheduling (or rescheduling) the day?

If you answered yes to three or more of these questions, chances are your child's schedule is too full and is in need of a change. Here are some things you might want to consider:

- Does my child have one or two hours of free time each day?
- Does she have time to go outside to explore and play?

- How often do we go to bookstores and libraries and hang out?
- Do we make time to sit and reflect?
- Are there art supplies, toys, blocks, games, and books available around the house?
- Can my child dig in the yard, plant gardens, and make mud pies?
- Do I make an effort to schedule occasional visits to art galleries, science museums, the exploratorium (hands-on science), or the aquarium as a way to keep my child connected to the things that interest her the most?
- Do we ever have breakfast in bed together? Snuggle to watch a movie? Sit and drink lemonade on the porch? Just talk?

If these simple activities seem like rare occurrences, consider creating more open time to do uncomplicated things that are genuinely pleasurable. Reduce the tempo, and instead of moving at a feverish pace, go with the flow. Encourage your child to hang out with you so she might learn to sew, knit, weave, fix her hair, build a castle out of pillows, camp out in the backyard, construct a homemade bug house, or do any number of activities that can be enjoyed at home.

Creating Sacred Spaces for Nourishing the Spirit

In my family, spirituality was expressed in a variety of ways. For starters, my father was a minister and my maternal grandmother was adopted as an honorary member of the

Cherokee Nation because of her amazing gift of healing. My mother, Anne, also exposed me to many spiritual practices—Native American prayer ceremonies and sweat lodges—as well as amazing experiences out in nature where I could commune with God as easily as I could listen to the beat of my own heart. And I quickly learned how life-affirming these activities were because they always brought me home to myself—and you can't get more balanced than that.

Don't be afraid to pray with your children or to engage in more spiritual activities. Sacred space is peaceful, safe, consecrated space where one can be authentic. It is essential to balance because it allows our children to experience sanctuary, a safe and peaceful place, and they know what it is to feel completely safe. In this space, their essences can be revealed. In fact, expression of their essence is encouraged by whomever is in that space with them: parents, teachers, and so forth. And they need not attend a mass or enter a holy temple or synagogue to experience a sense of wholeness, connectedness, and being close to the life force, whatever that means to them.

Today, with my own children, I often pull out my tarot card deck and have each person draw a card. This is just one way to help my children open to the richness of their inner life with honesty. The messages always strike a chord, and they provide an opening for each child to elaborate on any theme that touches his or her inner life. Reading the tarot also allows each of us the chance to hear everyone speak from his or her most authentic voice. I never cease to be amazed at the wisdom that comes from my brood and this is a great way for them to be able to open up and let their spirits soar.

Another very simple activity we do is to create a candlelighting ritual whenever one of the kids has an accomplishment (either a personal accomplishment such as conquering a fear, facing a challenge, or rectifying a mistake or any significant accomplishment like winning a soccer game, completing a special work of art, or doing well on a test or homework assignment). We light five candles in total, and as each one is ignited, we say a prayer of thanks, praise, and love especially designed for the particular child and his or her accomplishment. (The child may wish to contribute to the ritual with his or her chosen words). Then the celebrated child blows out the candles and receives a small gift (chocolate-covered nuts, strands of licorice, a little toy, a deck of cards, or a book).

Creating sacred space, where our children's spirits can be given expression and find repose, is one of the most effective ways to create balance. Children need to learn how to find their way back home. They need to learn how to locate their center in the midst of the centrifugal force of life. Otherwise, the imbalances can become larger and may create more serious problems later.

Determing Difficulties and Finding Help for Imbalances

Let's face it. No matter how well-adjusted our children are, no matter how confident, they will, inevitably, experience bumpy periods during the course of their lives. These troubled times may vary in their intensity and have a greater or lesser impact on our loved ones. Nevertheless, our children will need our love and support, our guidance and clarity to come through the difficulties in a healthy way—one that does not crush the spirit. As uncomfortable as subjects such as rape, incest, alcoholism, post-traumatic stress disorder, attention deficit disorder (ADD) and attention deficit hyper-activity disorder (ADHD), eating disorders, chronic depression, dyslexia, anxiety, phobias, and learning disabilities are to discuss and, if need be, come to terms with, it is essential that we, as parents, summon the courage to help our children when necessary. Whether the difficulties arise from physiological imbalances, emotional stress and turmoil, violence, or trauma, it is important to address them and take the time to help our children heal and make the changes they need to live fulfilling lives. It is my sincere hope that all our children's lives will be free of any serious, life-damaging trials. Yet, should they occur and become disruptive to healthy and happy individuals and families, I encourage you to educate yourselves and seek assistance from those who are intimately involved in the areas of concern: professionals, clergy, support groups, teachers, healers, physicians, therapists—whomever you trust has the knowledge and wisdom your children can benefit from.

When my son, Alexander, was in second grade, his teacher called me in because she was concerned about the gap that was steadily widening between his mathematics skills and his reading skills. He seemed to be having difficulty concentrating and sticking with the sometimes arduous process of sounding out words. His ability to recognize entire words was below his age group, and although no one was seriously worried, we decided to get a jump on the problem, hoping to prevent further disruption in his learning—and his good feelings about himself. Alexander's principal assembled a team that included both parents, Alexander's teacher, and the language-resource specialist who was affiliated with the school. Because I had been labeled with a learning disability around the same age as my son (to this day I am convinced that it was a result of my parents' bitter divorce and my emotional response to it), it wasn't easy to prevent myself from feeling anxious. However, I was confident that everyone in the room had my son's best interest at heart, and so we proceeded.

First, a horizontal chart was made on a long piece of paper in the front of the room so everyone in the group could see what was written. Then we began by listing Alexander's strengths. Next, we explored information specific to him, such as the fact that he is a spirited child (easily distracted, but not in the same sense as someone with ADD); he is a highly sensitive child; he needs a full eight to ten hours of sleep a night; he tends to have sinus problems throughout the school year; he divides his time between both parents' homes (60 percent with Mom and 40 percent with Dad); he is sensitive to sugar and milk products (they tend to make him hyper and aggressive, especially if he hasn't eaten any healthy meals in conjunction with these foods); and so on. The next column indicated situations in which his reading improved and he seemed more comfortable. Not surprisingly, Alexander, as an introverted male, sensitive to the comments of others, showed immediate improvement in his reading when in small groups and one-on-one. I had noticed this when my friend Jon's daughter, Sara, who is eleven years old, sat down with him to do homework. In column four we listed the "Areas of Concern," again focusing in on the most pressing issues: whole-word recognition, decoding, gap between reading and math, easily distracted, and feels tired. Last, we brainstormed as a method for arriving at simple yet helpful solutions to his reading "problem."

Since that time, both his father and I have made sure

that reading is basically an everday occurrence. During the summer months we enrolled him in a wonderful reading program where parents are welcome to attend and learn alongside their children (for information, call the Institute of Reading Development at [800] 964-2030). And, thankfully, Alexander is feeling more self-assured and is enjoying reading on his own more—and this is exactly what we had hoped for. But it is important that we continue to integrate his reading practice into everyday life so, eventually, it will no longer be viewed as a difficulty. I'm sure, by then, we will be facing other challenges. . . .

Granted, the difficulty faced by my son might appear to be small compared to more-severe problems faced by children. But I highly recommend the steps we took and appreciate the fact that others in our community reached out to assist us. It can be an effective approach for generating ideas and coming up with a positive plan of action.

Below I have listed a variety of difficulties, followed by resources that may be helpful in improving a child's quality of life. The purpose is *not* to prescribe treatment or to offer a diagnosis. Rather, I offer these descriptions in an effort to illuminate many of the problems children suffer from today in the hope that they can be dealt with and, if possible, eradicated or brought to a level where they do not hinder any child's growth and enjoyment of life. I cannot guarantee their effectiveness.

Post-Traumatic Stress Syndrome

Post-traumatic stress disorder can result from a variety of experiences: rape, war, violence, sexual abuse, divorce, domestic violence (verbal and physical), or car and other serious accidents (especially if violence or sudden death was witnessed). For the individual to cope or even to survive, the memory is put away, stored in a compartment of the brain, hidden. Although time marches on, the past trauma is carried forward, thus coloring present-day circumstances. It is as though the pain of the trauma infects what is taking place in the moment. Yet, in all likelihood, the person may not be aware of it nor is he cognizant of the effect he may be having on those around him. Until past wounds can be healed or released and brought to some kind of resolution, the individual suffering from post-traumatic stress syndrome will be plagued by the pain, hurt, and devastation of the past. As parent educators Jeanne and Don Elium attest in their book *Raising a Family*, "Until the emotional and phys- ical effects of the original event are released and integrated, we remain at the mercy of the past. Many, many people in our culture suffer from post-traumatic stress, because we do not know how or do not take the time to deal with the after-effects of sudden, critical changes in our lives."

Resources for Post-Traumatic Stress Syndrome

National Council on Child Abuse and Family Violence Help Line
(800) 222-2000

Childhelp/IOF Foresters National Child Abuse Hotline
(800) 4-A-CHILD

The Eye Movement Desensitization and Reprocessing Institute (EMDR)
P.O. Box 1010
Pacific Grove, CA 93950
(408) 372-3900 (helpful for trauma, anxieties, and phobias)

For information on rape and sexual violence, contact your local rape crisis line.

National Coalition for Family Justice
Monica Getz, President
821 Broadway
Irving-on-the-Hudson, NY 10533
(914) 591-5753

Life Transformation Process
David Pasikov, M.A.
(303) 443-0694

Echoes of the Ancestors
Malidoma Some, Ph.D., and Sobonfu Some
4400 Keller Avenue, Suite 260
Oakland, CA 94605-4505
(510) 482-1097
Workshops offered: "Grief and Ritual," "Dressing the Wounds of Human Relationships," "Ritual," "Healing and Art," and "Ritual and Sacred Space."

Recommended Reading for Post-Traumatic Stress Syndrome
Post Traumatic Stress Disorder: The Victim's Guide, by Raymond B. Flannery Jr., Ph.D. New York: Continuum, 1992.
The Courage to Heal: A Guide for Women Survivors of Child Sexual Abuse, by Ellen Bass and Laura Davis. New York: Harper & Row, 1988.
Eye Movement Desensitization and Reprocessing, by Francine Shapiro. New York: Guilford Press, 1995.

Attention Deficit Disorder (ADD) and Attention Deficit Hyperactivity Disorder (ADHD)

As the names suggest, ADD and ADHD are disorders in which the person has difficulty focusing and carrying through on projects, thoughts, and simple things like daily routines. Because of an underactive frontal-orbital cortex of the brain, a variety of symptoms can result: short attention span, impulsivity, difficulty finishing tasks and projects (yet with an urge to begin many), difficulty with order and prioritization, tendency to daydream and get lost in fantasy, hyperactivity, and a tendency to want instant gratification. Those with ADHD are particularly prone to acting out and quite literally can't sit still. As one little boy who was correctly diagnosed with ADHD said, "I feel like a train is running through my body!" Those adults with ADD or ADHD often turn to alcohol, drugs, or exhausting exercise routines as a way to produce a sense of calm, albeit a temporary one.

Remember, those with ADD or ADHD are often highly intelligent, talented, and creative. Yet, because of constant discipline or being told that they could cooperate if they only wanted to, feelings of shame and problems with confidence may result. Creating a simpler, more consistent lifestyle is extremely beneficial, as is respecting the ADD or ADHD child's need to move, even if it is just to get up to walk to and from the bathroom at school. Combining movement and exercise with sustained focus can do wonders. Limiting television viewing, computer involvement, and video games as well as cutting out refined sugar, chemical additives, and processed food can be part of an effective treatment plan. And, if necessary, medication can assist children who are accurately diagnosed. I caution parents about diagnosis and medication because ADD or ADHD can be an incorrect diagnosis of a spirited, adventuresome, or highly creative and energetic child. Unfortunately, there is evidence that suggests that ADD/ADHD have been used as a catchall label for the convenience of a few exasperated, overscheduled parents who are primarily interested in sedating their children instead of making constructive changes in their lifestyle to help their children develop beyond the restrictions of their biochemical imbalances. Also, be wary of unskilled health practitioners who are uncertain about the root and proper cause of the problem. Just because a child may exhibit some of the qualities of ADD/ADHD does not mean he has the disorder. However, if you and your family are constantly plagued with a child whose perceptions change rapidly, who cannot maintain a focus on the needs of others, and is very unreliable even though he is well-meaning, it is worth checking into, for everyone's sake. Like all difficulties that arise, remember: the best thing you can do is educate yourself and be an advocate for your child.

Resources for ADD and ADHD

AADF (Adult Attention Deficit Foundation)
132 North Woodward Avenue
Birmingham, MI 48009
(313) 540-6335

CHADD (Children with Attention Deficit Disorder)
1859 North Pine Island Road, Suite 185
Plantation, FL 33322
(305) 587-3700

Recommended Reading for ADD or ADHD

Driven to Distraction, by E. Hallowell and J. Ratey. New York: Pantheon Books, 1994.

Right-Brained Children in a Left-Brained World: Unlocking the Potential of Your ADD Child, by Jeffrey Freed, M.A.T. and Laurie Parsons. New York: Simon & Schuster, 1997.

You Mean I'm Not Lazy, Stupid, or Crazy?!, by K. Kelly and P. Ramundo. New York: Simon & Schuster, 1993.

Windows into the ADD Mind: Understanding and Treating Attention Deficit Disorders in the Everyday Lives of Children, Adolescents, and Adults, by Daniel G. Amen. Fairfield, Calif.: Mindworks, 1997.

The Myth of the ADD Child: Fifty Ways to Improve Your Child's Behavior and Attention Span Without Drugs, Labels or Coercion, by Thomas Armstrong. New York: Plume, 1997.

Help for the Hyperactive Child: A Good-Sense Guide for Parents of Children with Hyperactivity, Attention Deficits, and Other Learning Problems, by William G. Crook. Jackson, Tenn.: Professional Books, 1991.

Eagle Eyes: A Child's View of Attention Deficit Disorder, by Jeanne Gehret. Fairport, New York: Verbal Images, 1991.

The "Putting on the Brakes" Activity Book for Young People with ADHD, by Patricia O. Quinn. New York: Magination, 1988.

Dyslexia and Learning Disabilities

Dyslexia is usually thought of as a reading or writing problem because many dyslexics systematically rearrange letters and sounds. Although this is one of the common aspects of dyslexia, it is not the only one. Those with dyslexia often experience a disorientation that can affect the senses of hearing, balance, movement, vision, and time. Dyslexics can have difficulty listening, and they may not seem to absorb what is being said. Reading and writing problems can be further exacerbated by the fact that nausea and dizziness can occur, making it almost impossible to concentrate and remain focused. It is not unusual for dyslexics to be distracted. In addition, time may be irrelevant, and as a result, they are often late. Under these conditions, it is easy to see why children with dyslexia have a negative self-image and often do poorly in school. Like other children with learning disabilities, the struggle to learn can far outweigh the rewards. The constant feeling of being overwhelmed and unable to comprehend what is being asked of you is a fertile environment for feelings of self-doubt, believing you are dumb or stupid, and experiencing excessive anger or rage. It isn't unusual for dyslexics and those with learning abilities to think of themselves as failures.

The good news is that recent research is finding ways to unlock the potential of children (and adults) who experience these disabilities. In fact, discoveries about the brain and the different ways in which individuals learn have shed light on the natural talents of dyslexics and those who may have learning disabilities simply because of emotional blocks or their unique learning styles. One artist I know seems to function better in the world of symbols and design, which is clearly reflected in his photographs and stone carvings. He still has trouble writing his own name, but he has learned to fashion a life that supports his talents instead of degrading or punishing him for the skills he lacks.

Much help is available. Seek it out.

Resources for Dyslexia and Learning Disabilities

Otton Dyslexic Society
8600 LaSalle Road, Chester Building, Suite 382
Baltimore, MD 21204
(800) ABC-D123

Recommended Reading for Dyslexia and Learning Disabilities

The Gift of Dyslexia: Why Some of the Smartest People Can't Read and How They Can Learn, by Ronald D. Davis. San Juan Capistrano, Calif.: Ability Workshop Press, 1994.

The Spatial Child, by John Philo Dixon. Springfield, Ill.: Charles C. Thomas, 1983.

Frames of Mind: The Theory of Multiple Intelligences, by Howard Gardner. New York: Basic Books, 1993.

Multiple Intelligences: The Theory in Practice, by Howard Gardner. New York: Basic Books, 1993.

Inside the Brain: Revolutionary Discoveries of How the Mind Works, by Ronald Kotulak. Kansas City, Mo.: Andrews and McMeel, 1997.

In the Mind's Eye: Visual Thinkers, Gifted People with Learning Difficulties, Computer Images, and the Ironies of Creativity, by Thomas G. West. Buffalo, New York: Prometheus, 1991.

Unicorns Are Real: A Right-Brained Approach to Learning, by Barbara Meister Vitale. New York: Warner, 1994.

Hearing Equals Behavior, by Guy Berard, M.D. New Canaan, Conn.: Keats Publishing, 1993.

How Children Fail, by John Holt. New York: HarperCollins, 1995.

Alcoholism

Alcoholism is a social disease that is on the rise. It has a major impact on sound family functioning because, as a depressant, it works to distance the drinker from his emotions, thus preventing him from dealing constructively with the life events, fears, hurts, and pains that he is attempting to numb. Although alcohol affects different people in different ways—some drinkers become rageful; others are "happy drunks"—the alcoholic is not the only one who suffers. Family members are often ashamed of the alcoholic's behavior; they walk on eggshells in an attempt to stop "alcoholic episodes" such as sloppy drunken states, verbal or physical abuse, and so on. Children and other family members spend a good deal of their time worrying about what the alcoholic is going to do next. Questions like this interfere with their lives. Their anxiety, fear, and shame escalate. They feel unsafe in their homes and try to compensate and cope in a variety of ways that, in the end, run counter to their emotional, spiritual, and psychological well-being.

Unfortunately, statistics show that alcoholism in youths is on the increase, especially among boys and young men. The good news is that there are a variety of well-established organizations, hospitals, and alternative healing methods that have been very successful, affording the alcoholic and those close to him a new lease on life.

Resources on Alcoholism

Alcoholics Anonymous General Service Office
Grand Central Station
P.O. Box 459
New York, NY 10163
(212) 870-3400

Al-Anon Alateen Information Services
(800) 344-2666

Recommended Reading on Alcoholism
It Will Never Happen to Me, by Claudia Black, M.A.C.
   Denver, Colo.: Balantine Books, 1982.
Codependent No More, by Melodie Beattie, New York:
   HarperCollins, 1996.
*A Gentle Path Through the Twelve Steps: The Classic Guide
   for All People in the Process of Recovery,* by Patrick
   Carnes, Ph.D., Center City, Minn.: Compcare Publica-
   tions, 1996.
A Woman's Way Through the Twelve Steps, by Stephanie S.
   Covington, Ph.D., Center City, Minn.: Hazelden,
   1994.

Eating Disorders

Eating disorders are prevalent among teenage girls. However, they are not restricted to this age group, and there is a
rise in the number of boys affected by weight problems,
anorexia, and bulimia. It is not surprising when we consider
our country's preoccupation with physical appearance.
Commercials hold up certain body types as the ideal regardless of whether the models chosen are in the minority of the
population or not. As Jeanne and Don Elium put it in their
book *Raising a Family,* "Our children become so consumed
by whether they measure up (or down) in outer appearance
that they lose touch with what matters on the inside. Effective treatment for anorexia, bulimia, and other eating disorders is available and seeking help at the first sign of trouble
is vital. Prolonged effects can be lethal." The signs to watch
for follow:

- An obsession with food
- An obsession with weight loss or gain
- Self-deprecating comments about one's body
- A weight gain or loss of ten to fifteen pounds within a short period of time (three to six weeks)
- An emotional body image that is unrealistic, for example, a child who constantly complains she is gross and fat when she is actually thin or normal in size

Maintaining healthy eating habits, regular exercise, and methods of soothing and nurturing one's body and spirit (e.g., meditation, yoga, hot mineral baths, massage) is one of the best methods for preventing eating disorders. Encouraging a positive self-image and avoiding comments about another's looks are also helpful when promoting a positive self-image. If, however, you suspect problems, don't be afraid to find help at the first opportunity.

Resources for Eating Disorders

Anorexia Nervosa and Related Eating Disorders (ANRED)
www.anred.com

Shapedown Weight Management Program for Children and Teens
Balboa Publishing
11 Library Place
San Anselmo, CA 94960
(415) 453-8886

Recommended Reading for Eating Disorders
Living with Anorexia and Bulimia, by James Morrey. New York: St. Martin's Press, 1993.

Fat Is a Family Affair, by Judi Hollis. Center City, Minn.:
  Hazelton Foundation, 1985.
*Feeding the Hungry Heart: The Experience of Compulsive
  Eating,* by Geneen Roth. New York: Plume, 1993.
Losing Your Pounds of Pain, by Doreen Virtue, Ph.D.
  Carlsbad, Calif.: Hay House, 1994.

Chronic Depression

All of us go through times when we feel sad about losses and
changes. We may even grieve the death of a loved one or the
fact that a marriage ended. However, when depression
begins to last with no end in sight, it is important to reach
out for assistance. Chronic depression is a long-term condi-
tion that spirals downward into feelings of intense sorrow,
hopelessness, and despair. Those experiencing chronic
depression lose their love for life. They become disinterested
in things they were passionate about previously. Their emotions feel stuck and their energy is extremely low to the
point where the events and responsibilities of everyday life
are overwhelming. If left untreated, chronic depression can
lead to suicide or a feeling of wanting to die because it is too
difficult to cope.

Depression is not reserved for adults. Children can and
do experience bouts with it. If it persists, get help immediately. Depression can have situational causes or can be the
result of biochemical imbalances (some of these imbalances
can occur as a result of prolonged stress, too many losses at
once or in a short period of time, or from a traumatic or
violent event). Signs to watch for, even in infants:

- *Withdrawal* (physically, emotionally, and psychologi-
  cally) as characterized by a vacant, listless appearance
  and little-to-no verbalizing, no touching, and

avoiding human connection. (Some children may
choose only to relate to animals when they feel
depressed.)

- *Irritability.* Family members may feel as though they
  are always on guard when someone is depressed.
  Because rapid mood swings are common, others can
  be fearful about approaching the depressed person
  because they could get yelled at for the most
  insignificant thing or for no reason at all. Any
  remorse only compounds the problem, leading to a
  vicious cycle of feeling bad.
- *Excessive sleeping*, TV watching, or "getting lost" in a
  book or project and staying there. Have you ever
  seen a sick cat retreat into a safe place and literally sit
  still for days, only leaving its chosen spot for a few
  minutes to eat or use the catbox? Depressed children
  find safe places to retreat. They may need inordinant
  amounts of sleep. They may engage in movie mara-
  thons or hideout in the world of books for awhile. It
  is important to respect these coping methods. In
  some cases, this behavior can create healing, allowing
  children time to grieve, deeply reflect on an event or
  loss, or temporarily still the flood of emotions they
  feel until they are better able to deal with them—on
  their own timing. Of course, if this behavior lasts for
  months, you might need to help your children slowly
  make the transition back to normal living. The
  important thing is to learn to differentiate between
  the times a child needs to go deep inside for
  solitude—as one way to heal pain or chronic stress
  and simply rejuvenate—as opposed to continually
  shutting out others (and the world around him).

Resources for Chronic Depression

Depression and Related Affective Disorders (DRADA)
Johns Hopkins University School of Medicine
Meyer 3-181
600 North Wolfe Street
Baltimore, MD 21224
(410) 955-5000

American Association of Suicidology
2459 South Ash
Denver, CO 80222
(303) 692-0985

Recommended Reading for Chronic Depression
Listening to Prozac, by Peter D. Kramer, M.D. New York:
   Penguin, 1993.
Natural Prozac, by Dr. Joel Robertson with Tom Monte.
   New York: HarperCollins, 1997
Potatoes Not Prozac, by Kathleen DesMaisons, Ph.D. New
   York: Simon & Schuster, 1998.
What to Do When Someone You Love Is Depressed, by
   Mitch Golant and Susan K. Golant. New York: Henry
   Holt, 1998.
Breaking the Patterns of Depression, by Michael D. Yapko,
   Ph.D. New York: Doubleday and Company, 1998.
*The Depression Workbook: A Guide for Living with Depres-
   sion and Manic Depression,* by Mary Ellen Copeland,
   M.S. Oakland, Calif.: New Harbinger Publications,
   1992.
Meditations for Overcoming Depression, by Joan Borysenko
   (available in audio cassette only). Order audio from
   The Courage to Change (800) 440-4003.

Anxieties and Phobias

I include this section because of recent studies on the increasing numbers of children who are experiencing anxiety—and some of these anxieties eventually translate into full-blown phobias. Dr. M. Scott Peck, best known for his bestseller *The Road Less Traveled*, has, in recent years, coined the phrase "the Age of Anxiety." With so many changes taking place at such a rapid rate, it is not difficult to see why people are feeling uneasy. Job security is not what it used to be, public schools are struggling to keep up with children's needs amid tight budgets, gang activity covers the news, and so on. The things we once counted on as anchors, the communities that used to keep us buoyant, are no longer as stable. In addition, as I will discuss throughout the book, children are being pressured to keep up with too much stimulation and too many activities and classes, and they often have less time with family members and loved ones who make them feel secure and protected. To live in a perpetual state of anxiety, never knowing when an anxiety attack is going to occur, can be disruptive and disturbing. Treatment involves a gradual desensitizing of the anxiety in conjunction with releasing the emotions or trauma of the past.

Resources for Anxieties and Phobias

Anxiety Disorders Association of America
6000 Executive Boulevard, Suite 513
Rockville, MD 20852
(301) 231-9350
www.adaa.org

National Institute of Mental Health
(800) 64-PANIC (request a packet from the
information line)

Anxiety Disorders
79 Madison Avenue, Third Floor
New York, NY
(212) 213-0909

Internet Mental Health
www.mentalhealth.com

Stress and Anxiety Research Society
http://star-society.org

Recommended Reading for Anxieties and Phobias
Don't Panic, by R. Reid Wilson. New York: Harper &
    Row, 1986.
Anxiety Disorders and Phobias, by Aaron Beck and Gary
    Emery. New York: Basic Books, 1985.
The *Anxiety and Phobia Workbook*, by Edmund J. Bourne,
    Ph.D. 2nd ed., Oakland, Calif.: New Harbinger, 1995.

Allergies

Allergies can have a negative impact on children's lives. The
symptoms of allergies—fatigue, sore throats, sinus and
breathing problems, watery eyes, and a wearing down of the
immune system, making children more susceptible to colds,
flus, and other ailments—can make it difficult for children
to participate in sports, hayrides, picnics, and a variety of
other activities. In fact, allergies can interfere with school

when chronic fatigue and not feeling well are almost a daily drill. And, as I've mentioned before, allergies to food can create behavior problems, imbalances in blood-sugar levels, and hyperactivity. Often, allergies are very treatable. Alternative and complementary medicine are as effective as more traditional methods. Homeopathic medicine, chiropractic, naturopathic, and a new approach called "Nambudripad Allergy Elimination Technique" are readily available. Look ahead to the section on health (Chapter 7) for alternative resources. Additional resources follow:

Resources for Allergies

Asthma and Allergy Foundation of America
1125 15th Avenue NW, Suite 502
Washington, DC 20005
(202) 466-7643
(800) 7-ASTHMA

Recommended Reading for Allergies

The Best Guide to Allergy, by Nathan D. Schultz, M.D.,
    Allan V. Giannini, M.D., and Terrence T. Chang, M.D.
    2nd ed., Amherst, Mass.: Pedipress, 1994.

Food and Mood, by Elizabeth Somer, Ph.D. New York:
    Henry Holt, 1995.

Natural Way, "Stress Reduction: Take Time Out for a
    Free Day," by Andrew Scrivani, July/August 1997,
    p. 40.

Raising a Family, by Jeanne Elium and Don Elium.
    Berkeley, Calif.: Celestial Arts, 1994.

The Road Less Traveled, by M. Scott Peck. New York:
    Simon & Schuster, 1998.

Sugar Blues, by William Duffy. New York: Warner Books, 1993.

Fortunately, not all imbalances are as serious as those listed above. However, as parents and mentors, we must address all types of imbalances. Not only can we help our children to live happier, healthier lives, but we can take the necessary steps to prevent the more debilitating forms of physical, emotional, psychological, and spiritual imbalances from occurring.

3

Your Child's Unique Temperament

Children are as unique and individual as the stars in the galaxy. Yet, until recent years, the majority of child-rearing practices and the many volumes of professional advice have approached children as though they were basically the same. Today, we know better. Children are as different as their fingerprints, and a large part of how they learn, how they approach the world, how they think about themselves, and what interests them is determined by temperament. In fact, as parents are becoming increasingly more aware, temperament can be a guiding compass when it comes to raising our children. Instead of expecting each child to conform to external dictates, learning to piece together the various aspects of our children's temperaments can help us to more successfully know when to introduce a variety of structured experiences and when to pull back and simply hang out at home or in the park, allowing their senses to be stimulated by play. In addition, understanding temperament can assist us in determining our children's individual needs. Simply put, what one child may need, another may not. Particular activities that stimulate and excite one child may cause another to withdraw. Conversely, certain activities our children may find fun and challenging may overwhelm us, or we may find them completely unappealing and, as a result, we may attempt to direct our children away from their favorite endeavors erroneously.

As parents, we must be able to make these distinctions based on knowledge about our children's inner natures. Tailoring our parenting skills to our children's temperaments helps us to avoid unnecessary power struggles and trite conflicts when we could be enjoying our children's company and guiding them toward learning and activities that bring them immense joy and a solid sense of self.

I think Dr. E. Michael Ellovich says it best in his introduction to Paul D. Tieger and Barbara Barron-Tieger's book *Nurture by Nature:*

> Just as the gardener accepts, without question or resistance, the plant's requirements and provides the right conditions each plant needs to grow and flourish, so, too, do we as parents need to custom-design our parenting to fit the natural needs of each individual child. Although that may seem daunting, it is possible. Once we understand who our children really are, we can begin to figure out how to make changes in our parenting style to be more positive and accepting of each child we've been blessed to parent.

Temperament can give us important insights into how to interact with our children in a way that is most beneficial to them. It will help us not to force them or hold them back. Understanding our children's unique essence and not only nurturing but celebrating their individuality builds genuine self-esteem and confidence. What could be more important than that? Think of the times in your life when you felt as though someone truly understood you, understood your way of being in the world, accepting all your idiosyncrasies and eccentricities while respecting your opinions, thoughts, and feelings. Wouldn't our children grow and flourish more if we, as their parents, nurtured this profound sense of acceptance, love, and worth? Wouldn't we, as parents, feel less anxious about the choices we make for our children simply because we know them more intimately and can feel confident about our gut-level decisions based on that knowledge? Wouldn't we feel more comfortable saying "yes" and "no" to certain classes, activities, and experiences if we relied on our deeper sense of "knowing what is best" and knowing when to gather more information before we place our children in a situation hastily? Knowing more about our children's temperaments is one of the best ways to strengthen our understanding of who our children are, in their own right.

The Importance of Knowing Each Child's Temperament

One day while driving in my car, I was listening to a taped interview with Alice Walker, Isabel Allende, and Jean Shinoda Bolen, all accomplished authors and women of the world. The audience was asking very personal questions of each of these women, and I was touched by the openness and tender honesty contained in their responses. When it was Jean Shinoda Bolen's turn to speak, I heard a sentence that leapt out at me, and it is not difficult to see why. "My parents loved me," she said, "but they were not interested in finding out who I was." Then I thought of a parenting class I took on self-esteem. The instructor's first question was, "How many of you felt loved as a child?" A number of us raised our hands, but the majority of participants declined.

Ironically, coming from "good homes" did not automatically produce an adult who felt loved, respected, and cherished. Yet, as the members of the group spoke, I realized that they were echoing the same sentiments as Bolen. Sure, they knew they were loved, but they did not feel *known*. Their parents did not take the time necessary to find out who they really were—and this had left a hole in their hearts.

I cannot stress enough the need for children to be *seen* and *known* by their parents. It isn't enough to know our children's preferences and a few qualities about them. They need to be witnessed for who they are, deep down. As my friend David, a brilliant psychiatrist, always says, "Children need to be witnessed. Otherwise, their sense of self can be diminished, even eradicated—and this creates a deep sense of loss and a feeling of disconnectedness from one's true identity." This is why I encourage parents to explore the territory of temperament, yours as well as your child's, because, as Sarah Ban Breathnach writes in her book *Simple Abundance*, "The authentic self is the Soul made visible." Knowing more about our children's souls and allowing their particular magic to shine forth will help us to better direct our children according to their own natures instead of purely making choices based on the dictates of what is currently popular and accepted by society at large.

The Dangers of Ignoring Temperament

I recently heard a speech on the radio given by the new governor of California. I was pleased to hear that he had listened to the overwhelming cry of Californians for a better educational system, especially in a state of such great wealth and resources. Yet, as I listened, I noticed a tone that is becoming more and more prevalent in the United States. The governor used words like "excellence" and "improving test scores." He stressed the need for tougher educational standards and higher salaries for teachers. But not once did I hear words like "fostering a love of learning" "nurturing our student's talents." Instead, I felt like I was listening to a speech on getting tough on crime, not improving our children's joy of learning. I felt disappointed because, to me, it is a further reflection of the state of our union. We are anxious and frightened by the future, and, in response, we are becoming overly serious about learning, and bettering ourselves, and this is translating into treating our children as if they are little adults who, if properly trained, will "be prepared." (Whatever that means.) Soul needs, such as quiet, reflective time for active discovery of one's inner life, are very unlikely to be taken into account, and, under these conditions, overscheduling is very likely to occur. With today's overemphasis on future marketability, it is our job, as parents, to assist our children in keeping their core identities intact. Because, if our children's identities and feelings of self-worth are too closely tied to performance and externally measurable success, their true selves will be obscured, and, over the long run, they may lose sight of who they are, inside. Dr. David Elkind, author of *The Hurried Child*, has this to say: "I see too many kids at the college level who are sort of desperate because they always tried to do what their parents wanted them to do, and now they feel unauthentic."

Nurturing Individual Differences

In today's world it is difficult to imagine having the time to peacefully "till the soil" so our children will grow or having the energy to be attentive to our children's tempos instead of primarily fitting them into our busy schedules. Yet, as Dr. Ellovich puts it, "We all chip away at our children's sense of self in a multitude of little ways: the criticism and disparaging comments, our impatience, the times we hurry our children through tasks they are enjoying to do something we deem more important. It's the way we casually dismiss their interest or curiosity with things vaguely odd or seemingly inappropriate."

Knowing our children's temperaments can help us to organize our children's schedules, even when we are forced to rush to meet deadlines, in a way that is most advantageous to them—and us. For example, one child may feel overwhelmed by the getting-ready-for-school routine in the morning, and our continual coaxing and yelling at him to hurry may leave him feeling rattled as he attempts to absorb the lessons in his classroom later that day. Certainly, any lack of focus on his studies resulting from the morning's chaos will only make him feel more overwhelmed and as though he is at fault somehow. Because we may not be able to completely avoid the frantic morning pace, we could help this particular child by preparing his lunch the night before and making sure he gets out of bed early enough to make the transition from lucid dreaming to concrete reality. Instead of feeling inadequate and unable to cope with the hustle and bustle of the household, he can prepare himself for school at a pace that is more in line with his nature. And, respecting his own pace, he will build a bridge of successes that will extend into other areas of his life, giving him the confidence he needs to branch out and explore new things.

Another reason for nurturing our children's unique temperaments is that it helps us to assist our children in finding essential ways to rejuvenate, relax, and ward off the negative effects of stress. In our frantic world, this skill is essential for sane and healthy living. As Elaine St. James, author of the book *Simplify Your Life*, puts it: "We've been so imbued in recent years with the belief that we have to take advantage of all the opportunities out there. The urge to *do everything* complicates our lives. We've passed this complication on to our kids." By being sensitive to our children's temperaments and their particular needs, we will be better able to help them to find solace and inner peace. In the next several pages I will introduce three scenarios to illustrate how we, as parents, might help our children to find balance in a way that respects their individual differences.

Myers-Briggs Type Indicator

Although there are a variety of personality tests and type indicators, I find the Myers-Briggs Type Indicator to be a useful tool for describing important differences between individuals. It is used by educators, therapists, guidance counselors, child-development specialists, and corporations to determine an individual's strengths, qualities, and preferences. The Myers-Briggs personality test considers the following aspects of individual temperament:

- Introversion and Extroversion
- Intuition and Sensing
- Thinking and Feeling
- Judging and Perceiving

Introversion and Extroversion
The terms *introversion* and *extroversion* describe where a person usually draws his energy from: internally from solitude

and keeping the company of one's own thoughts for the introvert or externally from the stimulation of other people for the extrovert. Introverts may need to recharge their batteries after being in the company of others, especially large groups of unfamiliar faces, whereas the extrovert usually thrives on meeting new people and interacting with others. Authors David Keirsey and Marilyn Bates have this to say in their book *Please Understand Me*: "While the extrovert is sociable, the introvert is territorial. That is, he desires space: private places in the mind and private environmental places . . . Pursuing solitary activities, working quietly alone, reading, meditating, participating in activities which involve few or no other people."

It is important to remember several things in relation to introversion and extroversion. First, we all possess both of these traits to a greater or lesser degree, yet we must respect our innate preference. Learning where we draw our energy from, and how to rejuvenate ourselves when that energy is depleted, is an essential part of creating balance. Second, it is helpful to remember that we live in a society that encourages and rewards sociable, outgoing, and gregarious extrovert-like behavior. For this reason, introverts are often pressured to develop an extroverted persona for social situations that can drain them considerably. A child may be outgoing in behavior yet can draw his or her energy from solitude and reflection. As a parent, it is important to make this determination early on to make sure those introverted children receive the quiet time they need. As Paul D. Tieger and Barbara Barron-Tieger point out in their book, *Nurture by Nature*, "In a society that generally bombards people with stimulation, introverted children respond by withdrawing and then need time alone to process what they've experienced. Extroverted children tend to get overexcited by the onslaught of stimulation and need other people to talk with in order to make sense of it all."

Intuition and Sensing

The person who has a natural preference for the intuitive tends to be more of a visionary, seeing how things could be, rather than accepting how things are. Intuitives enjoy vivid imagery and often experience quantum leaps in consciousness, namely new and complex ideas or solutions to problems that suddenly appear in their minds. The sensate, on the other hand, places trust in factual information, focusing on the present and how things are rather than how they could be. Those individuals with the sensation preference often describe themselves as "realists." They are detail-oriented and practical-minded.

Thinking and Feeling

Thinking and *feeling* are the only personality traits that show a marked difference in gender. As you might expect, women tend to rely more heavily on the feeling preference, and men prefer to use the thinking mode. Those who prefer to use thinking to make decisions tend to use logic and analysis and give more stock to objective material. Feeling individuals tend to make decisions based on their own internal set of values and the feelings and needs of others. As Keirsey and Bates point out, "People with the F preference may have an advantage over those with the T preference for developing the less-desired preference. Formal schooling addresses the T areas far more than the F. Thus, those with a natural preference for F also tend to develop their T, while those with a natural preference for T do not have an equal opportunity to develop their F side, which may remain relatively primitive."

Judging and Perceiving

Judging is a desire to have closure to plans, to have things decided and settled, whereas *perceiving* is the preference for leaving options open so more data can be collected and additional options considered. In other words, those with a preference for judging strive for closure, and those with a preference for perceiving like to keep things more fluid and open.

Creating Balance for Different Types of Children

Now that you are familiar with some basic differences highlighted by the Myers-Briggs system, think about your child and his or her tendencies. Is he more introverted or extroverted? Social yet needs plenty of time to himself? Does he feel more comfortable with facts and certainty or does he always have ideas about how to create change and make things better? Does he need predictability in his schedule or does he prefer to be more spontaneous or, perhaps, a mixture of both? Is he emotionally sensitive or does he tend to think about problems and solutions?

It is important to remember that no child fits perfectly into any one category. However, the three profiles described here can assist us in learning how to better tailor our children's schedules to their individual needs, thus minimizing stress and creating more balance.

The Quiet, Sweet Heart

Picture a child who is quiet and introverted, highly intuitive and empathetic to others, feels things deeply, and although may not assert her need for structure, needs regularity in her schedule to serve as an anchor. She seems to feel the feelings of others before they realize they are feeling them, and if she risks verbalizing what she senses and others deny her perceptions, she may withdraw into her already vivid and rich inner life. Because of this child's sensitivities, she will need a consistent, calm environment. She would not do well going to a highly charged, noisy after-school program following her academic classes. Large groups and sustained social interactions can leave her drained and in need of replenishment upon her return home from school. Once home, she loves to involve herself in various art projects— collages, painting, sculpture—and she appreciates having one or two close people with whom she can share her passion and dreams. A small class where she can pursue her interests with other children would allow this type of child to blossom. In fact, she will come to count on the class as part of her schedule, looking forward to having time with others for a short period of time (an hour or two). If there are others in the class who are highly critical or if the instructor takes a harsh tone, this type of child can come to experience the class as stressful even though she thoroughly enjoys the activity. It is important then, as parents, to carefully choose teachers at school as well as class instructors. Otherwise, the tone of the adult can be too harsh and demanding for such a sensitive child, and instead of excelling, an introverted and sensitive child such as this might experience anxiety.

In the evening, during the school week, soothing baths with bubbles and a select group of toys for imaginary play help this type of child to rejuvenate and assimilate her day, especially if she has homework in her after-school schedule. Having books read to her, snuggling up to a parent while exploring topics of interest on the Internet, listening to soft music, and storytelling all stir this little girl's imagination.

If her parents are always on the go, it is best not to insist that she accompany them. Constant change, especially if she doesn't have time to recharge with quiet, can become very stressful and she may have trouble sleeping. If possible, she would do well to stay at home with an older sibling, a good friend, or a trusted baby-sitter. On weekends, going to museums and dramatic and improvisational productions will be wonderful events for her. Yet, at the end of the day, she may need to retire to her room to play with her toys, write in her journal, or try new styles on her hair. Although she may be self-sufficient, she needs time to be with others and feel included in family decisions and conversations. During one-on-one time—helping to prepare dinner, eating together, or making crafts—would be a good time to tell her about classes you've found at the community center that might interest her, and would she consider attending with you so she can check things out to see if she would like to take part? With this type of intuitive and feeling child, don't expect a definite answer right away. Give her time to mull it over and then revisit the topic in a few days. You'll know right away upon seeing the class if the tempo and teacher are going to be well-suited to her.

The Lively Intellectual

Now, picture a child who is highly intuitive, but instead of having a feeling preference, he has a thinking preference and is extroverted. He probably learned to talk early, and because his brain makes quantum leaps in connecting ideas, he may be impatient with others who are more methodical or those who display emotional sensitivities even though this child may be sensitive himself. He probably loves to learn and may discuss topics in an advanced way. In fact, he is likely to ask a lot of probing questions and can exhaust parents who think they can get away with simplistic responses. For this type of child, books, educational videos, natural history museums, reading, sifting through adult magazines such as *Life* and *National Geographic*, drawing, and playing with chemistry sets and mixing ingredients for brews or actual recipes stimulate his thirst for learning. He probably loves being the center of attention. However, he may not enjoy being snuggled or held unless he initiates it.

This type of child probably has difficulty focusing on the morning routine, as he tends to wake up with his own agenda and wants to get started on his projects right away. He probably needs coaxing and the physical removal of the spaceships he's building to focus on getting dressed, and eating breakfast. He probably enjoys school, yet he may be bored by certain topics and only wish to spend his time doing math or science and finding out how the natural world works. Supplying him with chemistry sets, ample cooking supplies, books, topics to search for on the Internet, and building materials at home is essential. Also, attending classes tailored to his interests—computer classes, science classes or camp, sports (for his high energy)—gives him time to socialize and excel (also keeps his mind busy). However, it is important for thinking children to make time to quiet their minds. Otherwise, their mind chatter can over-stimulate them. For some, this means engaging in a mental but meditative sport such as golf, tennis, gymnastics, or rock climbing. And, after the class is completed, tactile activities at home—playing with clay, playing in water, brushing the family pet—can soothe him. As parents, it is important that we not be fooled into thinking that such a bright and exuberant child needs to be always on the go. Helping him to slow down and saying no when his energy seems to be getting frenetic is highly important. Unlike feeling children, parental hugs may be rejected, and a more directed approach will have to be incorporated into family life. It can be as simple as turning off the fifth episode of *Hercules* or *The Nature Show* and inviting him to show you the castle he's built lately or the comedy routine he's been trying out in front of the mirror.

The Refined Dramatic

The third child gravitates toward the best life has to offer. She may always want the best doll, the best bedroom set, the best clothes, and, later, the best cars. However, she is generous with her things as well as her love—which she may express in exuberant and dramatic ways. Unlike some children who prefer to find sanctuary at home, this type of child loves to travel and finds novelty with the new. They find something they like about every situation they are in. Not surprisingly, this type of child can become bored as she seeks out the interesting things in life. At school, she will find topics that appeal to her and special friends to partake in her activities. It is good for a child such as this one to be offered a variety of classes and activities on a consistent basis. But this need not be every single day because a child like this can easily use her innate interest to come up with activities at home, in child care, with a friend, or with her parents. In fact, her sense of humor and witty charm make her very approachable, and she may collect friends around the neighborhood, not needing structured activities.

Like all outgoing children, she will need assistance from her parents to unwind at the end of the day. Simply finding a quiet room where she can spend time with the family cat will soothe her, as will a warm bath, reading with Mom and Dad about distant lands, and, together, creating a dream vacation. Like most extroverts, she will need time to talk about her day. So, simply listening to her stories and the day's events will help her to empty out her energy and fall asleep.

I hope it is obvious from the three examples that the ways to create balance need not be terribly involved. Be respectful of your child's need for solitude, one-on-one time, and enough, but not too much, social interaction. Use your evening routine as a wind-down time. Or, if your child needs to get out pent-up energy, go for a swim, take a walk, or play wrestle and then move into more quiet activities. Look for clues that tell you that anxious behaviors are being reduced and more-constructive behaviors and enjoyment are on the increase. Of course, every child is different, and you may discover unique ways to create balance according to your lifestyle. Trust your instincts.

I have provided two appendixes to help you determine temperament, including the Myers-Briggs Type Indicator system, in the back of the book. Use the systems provided as a reference to better understand your child as well as to get some ideas about finding activities and experiences best suited for each child. Knowing about temperament can help you to better assist your child as he navigates the complexities of our world to find his rightful place in the scheme of things.

Resources

Nurture by Nature, by Paul D. Tieger and Barbara Barron-Tieger (introduction by Dr. E. Michael Ellovich). New York: Little Brown & Company, 1997.

Simple Abundance, by Sarah Ban Breathnach. New York: Warner Books, 1995.

The Hurried Child: Growing Up Too Fast Too Soon, by Dr. David Elkind. Boulder, Colo.: Perseus Books, 1989.

Simplify Your Life, by Elaine St. James. New York: Hyperion Books, 1994.

Please Understand Me: Character and Temperament Types, by David Keirsey and Marilyn Bates. Del Mar, Calif.: Gnosology Books Ltd, 1984.

4

Meaningful Activities Worth Making Time For

By creating balance and allowing your child some unscheduled time, I don't mean to cut out all activities. Rather, it is up to you to decide how to best arrange your child's time in terms of her interests, but here I discuss some activities that I think are worth adding to the mix.

The Importance of Art

The trend in America over the last ten years has been to reduce the number of art, music, and dance classes in public education and focus on "the basics": reading, math, and science. Certainly, I sympathize with the small budgets most schools have to contend with these days. Administrators have difficult choices to make in terms of prioritizing what is offered in the curriculum. However, as the movie *Mr. Holland's Opus* movingly illustrates, classes such as music appreciation and band not only teach students about following notes and playing an instrument, but they are a special opportunity for students to learn about themselves and to express themselves in self-affirming ways. Pianist Bill Evans puts it this way: "The purpose of art is that it teaches us things about ourselves we would not know otherwise."

Art is an incredible expression of the mystery contained in each of us. Whether it is expressed through music, painting, drawing, poetry, dance, sculpture, or movement, its messages come from deep within. Our children can see themselves and experience themselves viscerally. Like those quiet, unhurried moments, when our children can freely and openly speak from their hearts and minds, art gives them another, equally powerful voice—one that helps them come to know themselves more fully and have faith in their unique abilities. As scientist Richard Lewis so eloquently puts it:

> There is a craving in children to receive images—to take from the world its many and varied pictures of itself. But just as they are willing acceptors, so too do they crave to give, to project onto the world their images, to bring those pictures of their minds to the companionship of someone who can receive and is able to acknowledge their gifts of images, who can help at the birth of that trust which enables the imagining self to communicate because it knows it belongs in the world, making and taking the world, its fullness.

As we settle into the new millennium, it is evident that art is becoming more and more separated from daily life. It is often seen as a luxury that can only be indulged in once all the work and chores have been completed. Its value has been diminished and eclipsed by our obsessive focus on technology and progress. Removing the creative, artistic process from our regular routines, reserving it only for trips to the museum and ballets at the theater, leaves us hungry for the food that art is. We forget the importance of soul food such as art and then wonder why our country faces the problems it does: juvenile crime, teenage pregnancy, and drug abuse. Eric Booth echoes this sentiment in his book *The Everyday Work of Art*:

> In Paleolithic times, art was a life-essential, right up there with food, water, shelter, sleep, sex and worship. Art activated and celebrated the important but invisible aspects of life that still hold people together. [Through the ages] the experience of art remained strong, active and important for average people. Artists were not seen as existing apart from the rest of society. Art was connected to mysteries and spiritual impulses, as natural a part of social cohesion as the parental impulse.

Far too often we look for the utilitarian value in art, measuring its worth with an inappropriate yardstick. Or we reserve it for young children, determining that as our kids grow, they must turn their attention to more serious considerations. Many parents deem art to be disposable as soon as their children begin kindergarten because they are anxiously preparing their little ones to compete in the world market. What is often overlooked is children's inherent need for joy and meaning (and this need is not for children alone!). Art provides both. Booth goes on: "Through practice, artists learn trade secrets. They pay attention to these basics as if their lives depended on them, because they do. These secrets are so powerful that they transform everyday, ordinary experiences into a wealth more valuable than bankable currencies. Artists make masterful use of the perspectives and skills we all naturally apply in unnoticed moments throughout our lives. These secrets have been rediscovered and passed along . . . and they are responsible for much of the good humankind has managed, and most of the joy."

Certainly, our children will learn whatever we put in front of them. They will dutifully learn facts and information and dive into new topics and areas of study. This is an essential part of their learning. Yet, if facts and information are not balanced out by the aesthetic, it eventually loses some of its meaning in terms of the human spirit. If it is primarily our children's intellectual development we are concerned about, consider these facts Booth brings up in his book: "According to scientific research, hearing complex music stimulates your spatial intelligence; making music increases synaptic development in the very young. A school curriculum that dedicates at least 25 percent of its time to the arts produces academically superior students, and using the arts in history classes increases students' retention of facts. It has been proven that good high school arts programs reduce dropout rates and absenteeism." Those of us who "do art" know its importance because we experience it. When we do art, we no longer have to ask about its value because its value is self-evident. Think about what comes out of your children when they work with clay or piece together a Lego structure. Or what about a child who takes the multicolored building blocks out of the box only to create a dramatic design on the floor that completely expresses his unique view of the geometric shapes captured in nature? What about the simple, yet touching poem a young girl writes to convey her feelings about and perceptions of her favorite grandfather's funeral? These are all treasures that illuminate the unique and special gifts housed within each of our children's souls. That they could bring this part of themselves out, whether in the simplest or most complex of ways, is the miracle of the creative process. In his book, *Poetic Medicine: The Healing Art of Poem-Making*, John Fox talks about the effect that poetry has on children and their parents.

> Many parents become more aware of their child's imagination, insight, and distinct "otherness" through poetic language. Assumptions and fixed perceptions are released as they open to a sense of surprise about who that child is. . . . For the child, knowing that he or she is genuinely seen and heard is an incomparable gift. . . . Children who feel they've been heard on a deep level gain faith in themselves. A parent's acknowledgment is much more than giving approval; it is a recognition of mystery in that child. . . . Being open to what your child thinks and feels indicates a willingness to allow them to emerge as a creative individual . . . on a unique adventure, with stories to tell about their journey.

As a close friend who is a practicing therapist recently confided, "I am a good therapist. But therapy is not my voice." Art gives expression and affords children (and their parents) the opportunity to speak with a power that is not always granted by our society. Intense feelings of anger, frustration, and disappointment (the uncomfortable feelings) as well as pure joy, elation, and love are often spoken best through the mediums of art. Their impact is concentrated and palpable, touching the heart, and circumventing the trappings of the mind. Never was this more evident than when I picked up a book of paintings done by Jewish children who had been separated from their non-Jewish peers and were awaiting transport of themselves and their families to the various German concentration camps. One need not be a genius or an art scholar to receive the power of these children's feelings of terror, horror, confusion, and hope as well as the bewilderment about their unfathomable experience. Often, our children, especially young children, need to "speak" about their feelings and experience in a way that captures its truth. And their voices may not come alive until the "words" are draw from the strokes of the brush, the lines of a poem, or the songs in our children's hearts.

Unrushed Time and Creativity

Ask any artist and she'll tell you that the creative process takes amazing concentration. You give yourself over to it and images, sounds, brush strokes, and symbols appear. Visions and dreams are carried out into the external world. And, as every artist knows, the creative process often has its own cadence and rhythms. One needs only to learn to listen and create the space whereby creative visions can emerge. It is no wonder, then, that artists often refer to the purity of the child's eye, the ability to approach the canvas or a piece of paper with unclouded openness. Richard Lewis puts it this way: "Children can turn anything into anything. For this gift we call them magical, born alchemists of the spirit. But they are more than this: they are the first real inventors—and each child in her own time invents the world all over again, as if it had never been made before."

To do this, children need unhurried time to focus and attend to the art at hand. Otherwise, it is impossible to allow the originality, wisdom, and purity of their work to be called forth and birthed. Those who do not understand the need for down time, time to do nothing, do not see that this is the gestation, the inner workings needed to bring the joy and spontaneity of art to life. Daydreaming is not a waste of time. Rather, it is an alternate state whereby artists reach into the other realms to bring forth their visions. To children, this is not necessarily a serious endeavor. It is one filled with pure love of the work because it is not separate from life. It is the voice of life itself. The infinite wisdom of the Australian Aborigines tells us that those who lose their ability to dream are lost. Children (and their parents) need time to dream.

Encouraging the Joy of Artistic Expression

Enrolling a child in a pottery class (or any art class) is a worthwhile endeavor. You might even choose to attend class with your child, and together you can enjoy the time to create. However, you need not invest large sums of money or rely on a community resource to incorporate creativity into your child's daily life. There are simple and incredibly joyful ways to bring creativity and art into the daily or weekly routine at home or in the comfort of your automobile. Below are some suggestions:

1. Ask open-ended questions and see what types of responses your children provide. They may surprise you. You just might see aspects of them revealed that you were not previously aware of.

   • What do you think the grass hears when people walk through it?

- What do you think the planets and stars see when they look down on us?

- What made you feel good about yourself today at school?

- If you could choose for us to do anything in the next two hours, what would it be?

- What would you wish if a genie appeared and granted you three wishes (my son's personal favorite)?

- What caught your attention today while you were playing outside? At school? At after-school care?

Your children may wish to write their responses down, blending them into a short story or condensing them into a poem.

2. While driving in the car—a place we often find ourselves—ask your children to give you or your partner two words, any two words, and you come up with a story. You can weave the tale into a nonsensical story or add a moral to it as a teaching story. Have fun with it. Your children will love the twists and turns the story takes (you will surprise them!), and they will marvel at the way you can integrate two very different words into one tale.

3. Sing songs in cars. Like most spirited children, my son Alexander gets bored with long car rides or repetitive car rides as we circle the city running errands. One of my favorite things to do with him is to come up with a song such as the Beatles' "The Continuing Story of

Bungalow Bill." But, instead of singing the chorus word for word, rearrange it into something like this: "Hey, Bungalow Bill, take your pill, Bungalow Bill. . . ." Then, start a verse based on the tune of the song that tells an absurd story about where you are and what you are doing. For example, "We went out grocery shopping with our dog and cats, too oo oo, the car was so full it felt just like a zoo oo oo. When we pulled into the lot, we noticed monkeys and kangaroo oo oos. We told them they couldn't come in with all their chewing gum and goo oo oo . . ." You get the idea. These songs can go on and on. Soon you will find that the children invent rhymes with their lyrics—and everyone gets a little silly, clever, and creative.

4. Create poems for your children. Children love to hear about themselves. Even if they feel slightly embarrassed about specific topics, they generally relish the thought of poems or stories written on their behalf. Here is a beautiful poem ("How the Days Went") written by the poet, writer, and teacher Audre Lorde:

> How the days went
> while you were blooming within me
> I remember each upon each—
> the swelling changes planes of my body
> and how you first fluttered, then jumped
> and I thought it was my heart.

Notice how this poem brings the experience of pregnancy into a softer, more sacred place, where a child can hear how much he was loved and welcomed into his mother's belly. To know a mother still holds these powerful and tender feelings for him is an amazing affirmation of his worthiness and the exquisite bond that is shared between them.

Think about the words you would use to express how you feel about your children and how each of them, in his or her own unique way, has touched your life. Then, write a poem for each child and read it to each of them. I have no doubt, whether they show it or not, you will melt their big hearts.

5. Write descriptive poems. Another type of poem that is wonderful to write for children and loved ones is a descriptive poem—one that incorporates all the subject's eccentricities, delightful quirks, and mannerisms. An illustration of this is a poem I had written for my mother on her birthday. It included the fact that my mother owns more pairs of shoes than Imelda Marcos and on holidays she loves to gather all of us around the player piano and sing old ragtime tunes. These are aspects of my mother that not everyone is privy to, and pulling those moments together into the concentrated mosaic of a poem brought her to life like a character in a novel. The references made her smile.

6. Experience Rainbow Mother art. I have a friend in Colorado named Caroline. She is originally from the South, and her attire frequently echoes this fact. Sometimes, she can look more Laura Ashley than Laura Ashley. Yet underneath that sweet exterior is a wonderful, wild woman who loves nothing more than to get her delicate hands into a block of clay. Sure, she might adorn

the dragon she has just sculpted with bright violet and yellow pansies from her abundant garden, but it is a dragon just the same. Or an alpha wolf, or a woman crying out in ecstasy, or a shapely mirror decorated with birds . . . You get the idea. The point is, Caroline collects and cultivates all the materials she and her children need to make castles for the gnomes, sprites, and fairies; individualized plates, bowls, and wall hangings; sculptures of the weird, strange, and beautiful; and flowered wreaths and colorful silk batik scarves. Instead of watching TV, her brood descends the stairs into the basement studio only to reappear with a magnificent creation, or "work in progress," as they say. For Caroline, art is an everyday experience, an experiment that has expanded her self-knowing as well as her children's.

7. Discover the tree of life. Create one by taking construction paper and cutting out a trunk, branches, leaves for the type of tree you want it to be: a sturdy oak, a flowing willow tree, a dancing aspen, or a red- and gold-leafed maple. Make sure the tree extends the entire length of your child's bedroom wall (you can even be extra creative and have the top branches "drape" over the bed by attaching them to the ceiling). Then take photographs, shells, favorite treasures, poems, drawings, schoolwork, locks of hair—any items that are representative of who your child is and what he has experienced—and place them on the branches of the tree. Next, ask friends, family members, teachers, mentors, and guides to contribute to your child's tree of life in any way they want. They can write a celebratory poem about your child; they can give you a picture of the two

of them; they can write about a funny thing that your
child said or did; they can draw a humorous picture (a
picture that represents unique and eccentric aspects of
your child), and so on. Add these to the tree of life,
being sure to ask your child about the exact placement
of each item (children often have specific ideas about
where things should go). Your child will be able to add
on a minicollage or pictures of newly discovered friends
and treasures as the years go on. The tree of life is a
moving declaration of who your child is by those who
love him most.

Remember as Eric Booth, author of *The Everyday Work
of Art* says, "Artists are nothing more than experts at experiencing." Take the time to create joyful and meaningful
experiences with your children through art and music. The
benefits will be immeasurable.

Sleep as a Meaningful Activity

According to recent studies, more than half of all high
school students are clinically sleep deprived. In plain language, our teenagers are chronically tired as a result of lack
of sound sleep. And we all know what happens when we
don't get enough sleep. Parents of newborns find out very
quickly what an effective torture method sleep deprivation
is and how it distorts perception and proper daily functioning. It is difficult to concentrate. Our thought processes are
slowed or impaired. We feel too tired to do what is required
for each day. In fact, we eventually lose interest in those
things we enjoy simply because we lack the energy. Randy
Rolfe lists the symptoms that are likely to occur from lack
of sleep in his book, *The Seven Secrets of Successful Parents*:

One falls asleep at school
Another craves caffeine and stimulants
Another loses his appetite
Yet another is irritable and startles at noise
Still another feels paranoid or depressed
One more starts fights at imaginary offenses

One reason children become sleep deprived is that they are not sleeping soundly. Broken sleep disrupts the much-needed REM sleep—the deep sleep that allows our bodies to go into a state much like meditation. Without this deep sleep, mood swings are common, physical exhaustion is noticeable, and lethargy and apathy take hold. Luckily, the solution is fairly simple if the problem has not gone on for too long: get more sleep! If, however, your children have been experiencing prolonged stress, there is a good chance that their adrenal glands may have developed what is called "an inverted pattern" whereby they are overworking at the wrong times. In other words, the adrenal system is out of balance. As a result, it wakes children up during odd hours because it is no longer aligned with a normal waking and sleeping pattern. Instead, it has been like a car with the accelerator pedal constantly held to the floor, totally throwing off its natural rhythms. Certainly, overscheduling activities during the day with few breaks and no time for quiet can create the type of sustained stress that causes erratic sleep patterns. Eventually, these will have a negative impact on children. In cases such as these, encourage nap time. Make sure your children eat a healthy diet instead of reaching for sugary foods, chocolate, or other temporary stimulants to keep them up and awake. Soothe them with hot baths, backrubs, arm tickles, and relaxing music. Make a conscious effort to assist your children in reversing an inverted adrenal pattern by allowing extra sleep—even if it occurs during the day, for the majority of the day. Rock them in hammocks or hanging chairs. Let them be couch potatoes. Rub their heads. Their bodies are trying to catch up. After all, sleep is an important activity for optimum functioning.

Stress Busters

Just like adults, children's stress can build up. Children, especially boys and more-active girls who are made to sit all day in a classroom, can feel tense simply from forcing themselves to do something that feels unnatural to them. Being in over-stimulating environments for extended periods can tax a child's nervous system. This is particularly true of introverts and chronically overextended extroverts. Although we, as their parents, may attempt to calm our children's nerves with relaxation, something quite different might be in order. Perhaps they need to get their wound-up, chaotic energy out by having a pillow fight, letting lose with boxing gloves, dancing wildly to out-of-control rock and roll.

An article on "Stress Reduction" that appeared in *Natural Way* magazine tells of Andrew Scrivani, a physical education teacher, who gives his students what he calls "a free day" of unabashed wildness. Mr. Scrivani explains it like this: "To the outsider it looks like thirty children going insane with every toy out of the chest. And that's exactly what it is, but with method to the madness. There are simple rules regarding safety, then I stand back and watch stress dissolve into laughter, running, jumping and various types of physical release."

Think about the ways in which your family releases tension. Below are some tried-and-true suggestions:

- Wrestle on a carpeted floor. Have a free-for-all that includes the entire family. Just make the rules of engagement clear.
- Let your young children jump on their beds (and into your arms).
- Jump on a minitrampoline or a large one outside.
- Buy an inflatable pool and fill it with water. Then make a water slide out of plastic bags or an old camping tarp. Be generous with the sprinklers.
- Play a game of chase. You be the monster and chase your children around the yard, the house, or through the basement. My favorite is to round up all the nieces and my son Alexander (he's been the lone boy for years) in my sister's basement during the holiday get-togethers (talk about stress!) and chase them, growling, "Yum yum, eat 'em up, eat 'em up!" I carry the baby around with me and we all go into hysterics—laughing, yelling, and screaming. I'm exhausted afterward. Luckily, the children are too!
- Dance around the house. Boogie in the kitchen. Sing, sing, sing.
- Go to the playground and play ball tag (whomever is "it" gently throws a ball to tag others) or hide-and-seek.
- Play "keep away" in the pool. Wrestling is allowed, as is screaming. No splashing directly in the face and eyes. Involve the whole family. Invite friends.
- Have a spontaneous battle. Let each child pick out a wooden spoon, rubber spatula, long tongs, or any other cooking utensil of their choice. Then divide up the cutting boards and baking trays (younger kids get first pick as they usually choose the lighter versions) and run around jousting and sword fighting,

using the cutting boards as shields. Again, safety rules must be clearly established. But this game can be so ludicrous that everyone ends up laughing and screaming with delight.

After the pent-up energy is dissolved, it is helpful to turn our attention to more soothing activities. Tactile activities do wonders. Consider these options:

- Play with clay.
- Plant in the garden or make mud pies in bare feet.
- Weave or sew; knit or embroider.
- Try simple arts and crafts such as beading necklaces, creating dream catchers, working with leather, designing jewelry, or glueing shells to a cardboard backing.
- Mix and cook batter. Roll dough for bread. Smoosh bananas for banana bread.
- Build with blocks. Piece together puzzles.
- Play board games or charades.
- Paint with watercolor on large sheets of paper. Outline your children's bodies, and let them decorate their self-portraits.
- Fill the sink with toys and soap bubbles for water play.
- Find an old camera or radio that they can dismantle and study the insides.
- Read together on pillows or in a favorite cozy chair.
- Make a tent with sheets and blankets.
- Listen to audiotapes of a story or lie down to listen to music together. Play the guitar or piano and sing together.

- Play with dolls in a dollhouse. Come up with interior design ideas. Design a house by poring through various magazines and catalogs.
- Cut out paper hearts and put a loving note on the back for someone special.

I'm sure you can come up with many more ideas. Simply including your children in your own hobbies and household crafts is more than enough. Or devote your full attention to whatever interests your children. They will feel your presence, and that in itself is a stabilizing force in their lives.

The Pursuit of Meaningful Activities

A talent is a gift from God; what you do with it is your gift to God.

—*Anonymous*

In the interest of keeping our children's souls intact, consider the following when contemplating which classes to enroll your children in, which sports teams to join, which piano or dance lessons to take, and so on. I highly recommend following your children's lead. Early on, they will show interest in certain activities, and it is up to you to determine whether to encourage them to stick with it or allow them to sample a variety of activities until they naturally settle on one (or several). Again, finding a teacher, coach, or instructor who is a good mentor and positive role model can mean the difference between succeeding and dropping out of a particular activity. A father I know in San Francisco worked very hard to make sure he could keep his daughter in ballet lessons, not just financially, but in terms of arranging rides to her class and changing his work schedule for weekend performances. She loved to dance and ballet was her favorite. When, at last, she received a scholarship to a prestigious ballet company, everyone was surprised that, after only a few months, her interest in an activity she had always loved was waning. Finally, her father got to the root of the problem: she loved to dance but she did not like the rigorous competition and the goal-oriented style of the teacher. "Ballet is my love," she told her dad, "not my life vocation." After searching the city, they found an offbeat, extremely fun, and yet challenging instructor who ran her own dance studio; and, as it turned out, she incorporated ballet with many other dance styles into her choreography and performances. His daughter had a perfect fit. She did not have to give up something she loved, and she learned that there was more than one way of participating in ballet.

Remember the film *Chariots of Fire*? It is based on a true story about two runners who went to the Olympics during the rise of Hitler's Germany. One of my favorite lines came when the young athlete explained to someone why he ran and how it felt. "When I run, I can feel God's pleasure." Helping our children to find meaningful activities is one part of helping them to find their purpose and passion, to find their voice regardless of whether it speaks through bone carvings done in the New Zealand Maori tradition, archaeological digs, athletics, dance, building, crafts, cooking, horseback riding, fine arts, mathematics, computer systems, teaching, healing, playing guitar, designing clothes, or whatever. Don't be afraid to check into unusual and out-of-the-mainstream offerings in your community. Not all children walk to the beat of the same drummer. And, like the father

in San Francisco, you may need to hunt around for varia-
tions on the same theme. Martial arts is a perfect example.
Many forms exist. Be sure you are enrolling your child in a
class where you respect the teacher's approach and philosophy. You might also look into workshops and more spiritual,
growth-oriented activities that you can participate in with
your children, especially if you do not adhere to any one
religious practice. Focus on your children's needs, talents,
and passions, and don't be intimidated by the pressures that
are prevalent today.

Not too long ago, universities wanted well-rounded
students (renaissance men and women). Now they want students to be specialized. Corporations continue to change
their standards. Like the stock market, we cannot accurately
anticipate the changes that will occur in a world that is
growing and evolving so rapidly. I once heard someone say,
"I'll leave the number of accountants, geneticists, lawyers,
doctors, graphic artists, marine biologists, and so on up to
God." I think this is good advice. Trust that you know
when your children are so focused and filled with joy about
their play or whatever they are doing that they are most
themselves. Trust that you will read the signals: liminal
moments when your children are so fully absorbed in an
activity that time ceases to exist (and I don't mean TV!).

Robert Fulghum, author of *All I Really Needed to Know
I Learned in Kindergarten*, tells a wonderful story that is perhaps my favorite example of what it means to trust our children to be who they are. As a young pastor, Mr. Fulghum
found himself in charge of a group of very energetic children. Thinking quickly, he organized a game called "Giants,
Wizards, and Dwarfs." "You have to decide now," the pastor instructed the children, "which you are . . . a giant, a

wizard, or a dwarf?" Just then a small girl tugged at his pants leg and asked, "Where do the mermaids stand?" "There are no mermaids," he replied, whereby she quickly informed him, "I am a mermaid."

As former first lady Barbara Bush said after relating this story to the graduating students of Wellesley College, "Now this little girl knew what she was and she was not about to give up on either her identity *or* the game. She intended to take her place wherever mermaids fit into the scheme of things."

Where do the mermaids stand? It is a pressing question. One we have to answer over and over, as parents. Yet, that is the beauty *and* the challenge of raising children. It is our task, then, as parents, to keep our eyes open to who our children really are, never automatically assuming they are giants or dwarfs, mermaids or wizards. Together, we can help them discover the yearnings of their own hearts and the ways to best express themselves, with joy and intelligence, in the world.

Resources

Mr. Holland's Opus, directed by Stephen Herek, 143 minutes, Hollywood Pictures, 1995.

The Everyday Work of Art: How Artistic Experience Can Transform Your Life, by Eric Booth. Naperville, Ill.: Sourcebooks, 1977.

Poetic Medicine: The Healing Art of Poem-Making, by John Fox. New York: Jeremy P. Tarcher/Putnam, 1997.

The Seven Secrets of Successful Parents, by Randy Rolfe. Chicago: NTC/Contemporary Books, 1997.

Natural Way, "Stress Reduction: Take Time Out for a Free Day," by Andrew Scrivani, July/August 1997, p. 40.

Chariots of Fire, directed by Hugh Hudson, 124 minutes, Warner Studios, 1981.

All I Really Needed to Know I Learned in Kindergarten, by Robert Fulghum. New York: Ivy Books, 1993.

Barbara Bush, speech at Wellesley College (Mass.), June 1, 1990.

A Question of Balance: Artists and Writers on Motherhood, by Judith Pierce Rosenberg. Watsonville, Calif.: Papier-Mâché Press, 1995.

Life, Paint and Passion: Reclaiming the Magic of Spontaneous Expression, by Michell Cassou and Stewart Cubley. New York: G. P. Putnam's Sons, 1995.

5

Creating Balance in the
Electronic Age

Technology occupies a large part of all our lives. As we grow comfortable in the new millennium, our reliance on electronics is increasing. Televisions, computers, radios, CD players, automobile "extras" such as automatic door locks and devices designed to regulate the vehicle's indoor temperature have become commonplace. Let's face it—technology is convenient *and* abundant. We must be careful to make sure that our children don't become excessive consumers of the latest technologies. Otherwise, it is all too easy for them to fill their schedules with television viewing, video and computer games, handheld electronic devices, and the constant stimulation that these electronics provide. Now, before you think I'm a "Kill Your Television" fanatic, let me assure you that I allow my children to watch television shows and movies (in fact, I'm a big movie buff myself). I allow them to play video games and spend time on the computer. Yet, as a parent, it is still my responsibility to moderate my children's interaction with electronics. Although mounting evidence suggests that some computer games increase spatial skills, they can also promote violence and virtual machismo. And although spending time on the computer can improve motor skills and introduce new ways of learning, it can also cause children to "lock in" with incredible concentration for inordinate amounts of time, making children deaf to instructions and mentally fatigued afterward. As with most things in life, electronics have pros and cons. Parents should pay attention to the upside and downside to make determinations about their children's use of modern technology.

Pay attention to the amount of time your child spends involved with television, computer games, and other electronic devices. Does your child prefer to spend the majority of his or her free time playing with computers or watching TV? Are you selective about the programming, commercials aimed at your children, and the types of computer games your child plays? Do you limit time in front of the TV? Or does it always seem to be blaring in the background? Do you encourage your children to find alternative activities and schedule nonelectronic times during the week? Do your children reflexively flip on a switch whenever they come home, travel to a hotel, or visit a friend? If so, you might consider cutting back as they may have become overly dependent on electronic entertainment.

Does your family opt to have time-outs from TV viewing, computers, radios, and handheld electronic devices? It is important that children learn how to entertain themselves, explore the labyrinths of the mind, exercise the body, and, generally, take time away from technology. Certainly, when we go camping or spend time at a cabin, it is easier to avoid entanglements with electronics. But at home, they are everywhere for our children to turn to when they're bored, in a rut, or simply feeling unimaginative. Consider designating a week or two as being TV free and/or computer free. During this time, concentrate on reading more often, visiting the library, designing your own computer programs (if your child is genuinely interested in the topic and may be a budding engineer), playing card games or board games, drawing, painting, sculpting with clay, going to the recreation center, going for walks, communicating, reading the paper together (the sections you find most appropriate), rearranging the kids' bedrooms, planning a trip, studying maps, looking up subjects of interest in magazines, arranging favorite photos into a collage and picking out a frame, sending a letter to your parents (the grandparents) to say hello, visiting the Humane Society and picking out a kitten or puppy, or volunteering some time at a hospital or nursing home. Obviously, none of these suggestions need be a long-term commitment except, of course, caring for an animal. Yet they will provide your children with portals into a variety of experiences—some of which may bring out qualities in your children you would like to nurture and help them to develop further. For example, I know a family who takes their black lab to hospitals so terminally ill children can pet the dog, love her, and tell her their hopes, dreams, secrets, fears, and private stories. At first, their children felt apprehensive and frightened by seeing others their own age who had lost their hair from chemotherapy, couldn't speak clearly due to multiple surgeries, and so on, but bit by bit, the father noticed how their son seemed to know just what to do to comfort the children he came into contact with. Instinctively, he would hold a hand, share a familiar joke, or simply instill peace in those around him because of his quiet and unassuming demeanor. For his parents to not only notice his ability to soothe others, but to actively support him when others might have dismissed this quality as being "weak," "overly sensitive," or "nice but not that important for a boy" helped him to eventually gravitate toward medicine and the healing arts.

Taking time to turn away from the TV, curtail time on the computer, and turn our children's attention to other activities and experiences truly enriches them in a way technology can't. Balance means enhancing our children's lives with electronics, not allowing lives to become dominated by them. Remember, as parents, we ultimately are in charge of the controls.

Is your children's behavior altered in any way after engaging with the television, the computer, handheld computer games, and other technologies? My children are definitely affected by computer games. The boys especially tend to act more hyper and sped up, they play fight with greater intensity, and they seem to have a difficult time settling down and taking other people's moods and feelings into account. In fact, for a time, they are oblivious to others and seem removed from the effects their behavior has on those around them. Certainly, this occurs in greater and lesser degrees, but it occurs just the same; and for this reason, I actively restrict time with electronics. Other parents have had similar things to say. Like published studies that deny any of the negative effects of sugar on children's behavior (often sponsored by the sugar industry!), it is highly unlikely with the recent boom in technology that anything but enthusiasm be expressed about the many machines and electronics in our lives. But, problems exist. There *are* downsides, and it is important that we take notice of the times when our children have "had too much of a good thing" instead of determining that their behavior is the problem. Pay attention and encourage your children to explore other options, ones that do not disrupt their normal disposition. If, however, your children seem basically unaffected, use your judgment to determine how electronics and other technologies will fit into your children's lives.

Children's Attention Span and Balance

It is not surprising to find statistics warning parents that children's attention spans are shrinking, going from an average of 22 minutes to 11 minutes. The fact is, television viewing and interactions with technology actively influence one's all-around ability to focus. For example, a child may remain intently focused on a computer game literally for hours. However, because of the fast-paced changes in scenery, such virtual challenges as being attacked by a huge metal shark, and flashing screens filled with virtual races, fights, or evil castles, children grow accustomed to constantly changing their attention within a larger focus. When in the real world instead of the virtual one they maintain rapid change of attention, this can become disruptive to doing schoolwork, carrying on a social conversation, or focusing on reading, writing, or solving more labor-intensive math problems. And, although I am truly in awe of the new, young minds that seem to be preprogrammed for abstract, spatial, and informational thinking, making quantum leaps in thought, I am concerned that our children may learn to live their lives at warp speed, missing out on those things that can only be experienced over time. In addition, in a society such as ours, mental prowess and power are deemed unequivocally superior to other kinds of intelligence, including what Daniel Goleman calls "emotional intelligence." Goleman points out that "our view of human intelligence is far too narrow, ignoring a crucial range of abilities that matter immensely in terms of how we do in life."

As you might imagine, emotional intelligence includes a variety of attributes woven together into a mosaic of being bright. In Chapter 9, I discuss the importance of developing our children's attributes not only because they contribute greatly to our children's success in life, but also because they incorporate other teachings into our children's everyday experience that can help them to be more balanced, truly well-rounded individuals. It is also my belief that the traits Goleman attributes to emotional intelligence—self-aware-ness, impulse control, persistence, zeal, self-motivation, empathy, and social deftness—couldn't be more important to cultivate in our children of today. Why? Because the cul-tural trends encourage just the opposite—immediate grati-fication, impulsive spending, smoking, eating, drinking—via intensified and targeted commercialism, each man for himself, and disenchantment with life because it may not always deliver. What does this have to do with attention span, you might ask. The answer is simple: those who learn to savor life instead of dashing through it will experience more connection with themselves and others simply because they will make time for it and, thus, they will feel more bal-anced (even if their vocation ends up being closely aligned with our futuristic technologies). In other words, while using the computer, TV, and other technologies, hyper speed may be in order. But it need not be carried over into human relationships (often expressed as intolerance and impatience) and the sheer enjoyment of taking in the perfumed scent of a rose, for example. Our children need the ability to pay attention—not only to the special and beautiful things in life, but to the things they may find difficult and those things that cannot be solved immediately.

Creating Real Time

In the 1920s Anne Morrow Lindbergh sat down to write about her own experience of being a mother, wife, and woman in the twentieth century. Her writings were eventually compiled into one of the greatest, most widely read books of our time, *Gift from the Sea: An Insightful Tribute to Bringing Balance into Our Lives, Both Inwardly and Outwardly*. She writes, "Woman's life today is tending more and more toward the state William James describes so well in the German word 'Zerrissenheit— torn to-pieces-hood' . . . she must consciously encourage those pursuits which oppose the centrifugal forces of today. Quiet time alone, contemplation, prayer, music, a centering line of thought or reading, of study or work. It can be physical or intellectual or artistic, any creative life proceeding from itself. It need not be an enormous project or a great work. But it should be something of one's own." Never were her words more true. Torn-to-pieces-hood is no longer solely the dilemma of wives and mothers. Children are experiencing similar pressures that will only increase with age as responsibilities grow. For this reason, teaching our children how to create *real time* is essential.

How does real time differ from unrushed time? Unrushed time enables us to slow down to the more natural tempos of life and living; it enables us to be more present and to be more spontaneous about the choices we make with our time. Real time goes a step further. It is closer to a state of meditation because it allows our children to suspend time through inward concentration. It allows our children to excavate places within themselves simply by harmonizing their energy, thoughts, and heart rate with a deeper rhythm (and they need not sit up straight and close their eyes!). Rather, real time can be created in a variety of ways: rituals, prayer circles, artistic expression, playing music, rocking in a chair, listening to the birds outside the window, arranging a bowl of flowers, decorating cookies—anything that brings you and your children's attention to a one-pointed focus. In short, real time is the opposite of what is considered cool these days: perky, sassy, always moving, always thinking, always sharp, clever and witty retorts, always ready to go, usually a bit frenetic and full of quips because real conversation takes too darn long. You get the idea.

Chin-Ning Chu, author of *Do Less, Achieve More*, concluded that America's business culture is so obsessed with being busy and perky that it ignores the value of being able to take time out and think about long-term solutions. Personally, I think this attitude has become pervasive in the general culture and children of today are encouraged to emulate this busy behavior because seriousness, focus, and pensive thought (the more meditative ways to use our mind and body) are viewed as uncool. Luckily, we can teach our children to be mindful of creating real time during their day. And if we engage in real time ourselves, they will learn that this is not a strange behavior; rather, it is essential for nourishing the spirit, mind, and body.

What constitutes real time? There are three elements: presence, attention, and authenticity.

Presence: Instead of being distracted and consumed by multifocuses, single focus—or *presence*—allows our children to hold a one-pointed focus without interruption. It doesn't matter whether it is during a conversation, staring out the window, or watching a fan rotate over and over. Whatever brings them into the moment so they can respond without distraction and bring their attention to whatever or whomever they are with at the moment.

Attention: One of my favorite poets, David Whyte, speaks about the incredible attention it takes for an artist, or anyone who is diving into the creative realms, to plunge to the depths in order to touch the genius and beauty within so it can be brought out for others to see. It is attention that allows our children to focus on their inner lives while, simultaneously, allowing the world to swirl around them without interruption. In Eastern philosophy, attention is described as having one eye turned outward and the other turned toward the inner landscapes. Attention, like presence, allows our children to be in the moment, open to fully living the richness of each and every moment no matter what that moment brings. Or, put another way, it involves attuning oneself to the many levels of awareness and adjusting ourselves in such a way as to resonate in harmony with our surroundings as well as those around us. I like to think of it as listening with my entire body and being. And, in this state, the superfluous falls away and the truly important things are easier to see.

Authenticity: Authenticity is what enables each of us, parents and children alike, to be the unique, multifaceted individuals we truly are. When we are authentic, we can more gracefully allow our children to be who they are, warts and all, because we are not so inclined to place a portion of ourselves in hiding. We do not simply show our best side nor do we expect that of our children. Rather, we allow ourselves to be real: to have a range of feelings, fears, preferences, doubts, passions, unique expressions, and our own ways of giving, receiving, dealing with stress, and communing with God (i.e., Higher Power, Universal Light, Nature). We are in real time because our beauty, our specialness, and our oddities can all be present at the same time. Thus, we do not divide our focus and dissipate our energies relating through a facade.

The combination of these three concepts are what I call real time. Most parents discover that when they become more present, focus their attention, and learn to be more real and authentic with their children, an amazing thing happens. Their children respond in kind. They open, share more, hide less, communicate more, and relax more. This, in turn, has a wonderful effect on us, as parents. We tend to find that because we are more in touch with our children, we are more in touch with our own instincts and deeply held values, and what we feel like doing for our children is often the best course of action. When it comes to deciding the many questions of balance, we can worry less and focus more, allowing solutions to emerge and trusting that, with the knowledge of our children, we can find ways to maintain equilibrium despite the centrifugal forces of today. Instead of wringing our hands, caught up in the anxiety of our age, we can trust what we understand about our children's pace, what they naturally gravitate toward; and we can make confident decisions about the amount of time spent with electronics and the quality of their interactions with technology. As a close friend recently confided, "The more I know who I am, the more obvious my choices become. My choices grow out of who I am, not the other way around." Creating real time will enable our children to know themselves better and to trust us more. Together, we can find the equation that works best for them.

Resources

Books and Articles on the Effects of Technology on Children

Endangered Minds, by Jane Healy. New York: Simon & Schuster, 1996.

The Disappearance of Childhood, by Neil Postman. New York: Delacorte Press, 1996.

The Plug-In Drug, by Marie Winn. New York: Viking-Penguin, 1996.

Evolution's End: Claiming the Potential of Our Intelligence, by Joseph Chilton Pearce. New York: Harper & Row, 1992.

Parenting, "Get the Picture," by Rae Jacobson, October 1994, p. 208.

Family Circle, "Who Invited Them into Your Home?" by Mary Granfield, February 2, 1994, p. 98.

Mclane's, "Toxic TV," by Joe Chidley, June 17, 1996, p. 36.

Parenting, "Can You Protect Your Child from the News?" by Jennifer Wolff, September 1997, p. 134.

Time, "Glued to the Tube: As regulators dither and the Power Rangers reign, new concerns are raised about what TV is doing to kids," by Steve Wulf, June 26, 1995, p. 66.

Business Week, "ZAP! SPLAT! SMASH!" by Paul M. Eng, December 23, 1996, p. 63.

Books Encouraging Real Time

Emotional Intelligence, by Daniel Goleman. New York:
Bantam Books, 1997.

Gift from the Sea, by Anne Morrow Lindberg. New York:
Vintage Books, 1991.

Do Less, Achieve More, by Chin-Ning Chu. New York:
HarperCollins, 1998.

Magic Trees of the Mind: How to Nurture Your Child's Intelligence, Creativity and Healthy Emotions from Birth through Adolescence, by Marian Diamond, Ph.D. and Janet Hopson. New York: Penguin Putnam, 1998.

Spiritual Literacy: Reading the Sacred in Everyday Life, by Frederic and Mary Ann Brussat. New York: Touchstone Books, 1996.

6

Nourishing with Nature

Nature is one of the best resources available for creating balance. Its grand expanse can swallow up our troubles; provide infinite sources of entertainment, pleasure, and education; and challenge us to be more authentic and open. Children are creatures of nature. They flourish in its presence simply because the trees, the sky, the mountain streams, and the ocean waves beckon them. The plethora of activities nature offers are not laden with rules and proper modes of etiquette. And, for a moment, or for days, we get to be in awe of the natural wonders that hold so many mysteries and miracles beyond our comprehension.

I remember years ago my dear friend Ginger Hinchman gave me one of the most incredible gifts of my life: a two-week white-water rafting trip on the Colorado River through the Grand Canyon. I had just left a stressful job in Washington, D.C., where I dealt with subterfuge, conflict, and inflated political egos daily. (Luckily, I also dealt with many wonderful, exceptional people, but the negative aspects of the job had worn on me. Talk about being out of balance!) Anyway, after a few days floating on the river, running rapids, and hiking through the side canyons, filled with sensual and dramatic rock formations, I could hear the voice of the river. I had been raised with Native Americans and mystical grandmothers, so the notion of hearing the spirit of the river was not completely foreign to me. But, what made me sad was realizing how my connection to nature had practically disappeared as I lived such a fast-paced, stress-filled life in D.C. Mind chatter had come to fill my head instead of the wellspring of my own being and my connection to the source. As a result, my thoughts were always focused on the next appointment, the next meeting, or the next task instead of allowing me to be still and in the moment. It had taken me several days, sleeping in the sand, looking up at the bright stars, and marveling at the unabashed moods and tranquillity of the river, to regain my nearly severed connection.

I once again discovered what I already knew: connection creates balance. I knew my place in the scheme of things, regardless of the fact that I had no job, a dwindling savings account, and no definite plans for the future. Because I felt connected, I was filled with the confidence and comfort in knowing that, no matter what, I would find the answers to these seemingly overwhelming questions, step-by-step. Why? Because, through nature, I was put in touch with the core of my being and I could hear the clarity of my inner voice.

Nature and Listening

Listening requires attention. And attention requires a quieting of the pulsing thoughts and outside bombardment of stimulus. Have you ever been out in nature with a group of urban children? It goes like this. First, they complain because, as they review their surroundings, the activities provided by nature are not automatically apparent. Tvs,

VCRs, radios, and other distractions are not readily available to them, and their reliance on these things becomes glaringly obvious. Then, after being shown around the woods or the mountains, they begin to emulate the tasks or activities they were shown by adults or more-experienced wilderness types. Next, they start to create their own things to do, often simple things like skipping stones on the surface of a placid lake, examining rust-colored moss as it clings to the side of a large granite boulder, or grimacing at the odd fascination of a banana slug creeping through the ground cover.

After several days without traffic noise, changing lights, TV, radios, crowds of people, honking horns, sirens, train engines, airplanes overhead, and so on, their little bodies start to take a new form. The muscles lose their tension. Their faces become more open and relaxed. They are less vigilant and anxious. And the silence is no longer something to be nervous about. On the contrary, it is welcomed because it gives them the opportunity to listen and to hear their own voices from within. Given enough time, these children begin to exhibit their own rhythms and cadence. They express their own original ideas instead of sticking to the comfortable conversation that revolves around television shows, the latest talk circulating around school, or other trappings of pop culture. They may miss aspects of the familiar. But, by the end of their trip, they have usually made an important discovery about themselves; they may know themselves in ways they were not anticipating. If they have had others—mentors, guides, peers—to share their revelations with and have received validation and encouragement, their visit to the great outdoors is nothing short of profound. A seed is planted in their hearts and, although it may be obscured by the onslaught of homework, television, and the city life, most of these kids know where to find it—especially if they have continued contact with someone they trust who can help them listen to their inner promptings (particularly when these promptings go against the predominant values at home, at school, or in the larger city culture).

Do your children have time to play in the park? Wander in the backwoods? Go camping? Do you make an effort to travel to places where the accommodations are simple and removed from excessive stimulation? Have you looked into ecologically-minded travel, close to nature as an option for family vacations? You might be pleased with the results. Not only are these types of vacations less expensive, but they allow the whole family to slow their rhythms and pull out of hyperdrive for a period of time. Don't be discouraged if you hear complaining initially. Listening, really listening, and going inside may feel unfamiliar at first but only if you and your family haven't been out in nature in awhile.

Camping

Camping is still one of the best forms of being outdoors. Whether you are camping in the woods of Wisconsin, on the Lake of the Ozarks in Missouri, on the ocean shores of Hawaii, in the Rocky Mountains in Colorado, or in the Kentucky countryside, the sounds, sights, and smells can quickly capture the imagination and calm the buzz of city life. Remember nights out among the songs of crickets, the hum of cicadas, and the chirps of frogs? Or, if you lived in the desert, you awakened to the shrill calls of hawks echoing off the rock walls? Maybe you recall coyotes howling at the moon? Moose calls in the wild? Rivers rushing in the background? The sweet scent of fresh grasses, the perfume of wildflowers, the unforgettable smell of a campfire?

When I was young, family and friends would trek down to Current River in the Missouri Ozarks. All day long we kids would play in the river. We floated on rafts, splashed, swung from ropes, let the current carry us for distances before we would swim back upstream, and constructed infinite creations made of sand. We were never bored. We never whined, "There's nothing to do." We slept soundly at night.

One day as I was lifting up large rocks that sat at the bottom of the river, a strange creature emerged. He looked like an oversize salamander with a shiny black body filled with yellow spots. I lifted the creature up and carried him to the shore where my stepsister and I spent the rest of the day building an elaborate home for this unusual animal. Quickly, we discovered that he needed running water to fill his gills, so we created a labyrinth of canals to bring the rushing water to him. When he emptied his stomach of a crayfish, we learned about his (or her) food source. Luckily, we had a friendly camp ranger who stopped by every night to check on us, and on this particular night we asked him about the salamanderlike animal I had found. As it turns out, it was called a hellbender. As we suspected, he was related to the common salamander. Not only did we get the opportunity to exercise our imaginations by building a rock and sand abode, but my sister and I learned about the natural sciences, firsthand! I have never forgotten that day or that strange looking hellbender. Camping affords our children the gift of happening upon the unusual and incredible secrets of nature. I highly recommend taking advantage of sleeping out in nature.

Planning a Family Camping Trip

Consider asking yourself some questions about the type of camping trip you and your family would enjoy. It is my hope that these questions will get you thinking about the kind of trip you could design to expand your family's horizons, explore new territory, and bask in an environment suited to your family's needs.

- Do you and your family prefer cold climates or tropical ones?
- If you now live in a different part of the country, consider returning to your place of origin so your children can discover other worlds. Would it be possible to take them back to one of your favorite spots?
- Would you like to spend less time in hotels and more time in tents and woodsy cabins? When you and your family go on vacations, do you ever spend time away from civilization?
- Have you and your family avoided vacations because you're afraid they will be too expensive?
- Did you know that camping vacations can save you money regardless of whether you travel in state or to another part of the United States?
- Have you ever considered setting up a special account as a travel fund? Deposits of $100 a month add up pretty quickly.
- Are you in contact with a travel agency that gives you personalized attention by keeping you abreast of reduced fares and ecolodges worldwide and can make special arrangements with travel contacts outside of

your area? You might want to look into such an agency. I highly recommend Off The Beaten Path in Bozeman, Montana. Agents Cindy Olsen and Christine Searle are excellent travel agents, specializing in a variety of excursions. They can be reached at (800) 445-2995.

• Do you have other families you can hook up with to go on camping trips, river-rafting trips, and other outdoor adventures? You can introduce each other to local campgrounds, hiking trials, and small-town vacation spots away from urban centers.

Remember, North America has many amazing places to explore: the Badlands of South Dakota, the beaches of North Carolina, the Florida Keys, the side canyons of the Grand Canyon (I highly recommend Havasu—Eden on Earth!), Yellowstone National Park, Yosemite National Park, Grand Teton National Park, the Smokey Mountains, the Appalachian Trail, the Boundary Waters Canoe Area in Minnesota, the hot springs in Arkansas . . . the list is endless.

On the other hand, if you and your family want to explore exotic lands in different countries, consider ecotents and ecolodges in the Caribbean (Mayo Bay on Saint John Island is wonderful for children!); ecograss huts near the Tulum ruins in Mexico; or Costa Rica, where you can introduce your children to scarlet macaws, sea turtles, toucans, tropical birds and fish, giant hermit crabs that actually have road signs designating their crossing paths, white sand beaches, Mayan and Aztec ruins . . . again, the list is endless. As a mother with a limited budget who has an insatiable hunger for travel, I have found that ecotourism not only is affordable, but I avoid competing with hoards of tourists and I am always in beautiful and undisturbed natural areas that offer children outdoor adventures, peace, and the freedom to roam. Think about it the next time you and your family want to explore the world.

Seasonal Activities

My editor, Judith McCarthy, told me about trips she used to take with her mother to the eastern seashore during the fall months after the beaches had been emptied of tourists. Together, they would make sand castings. To Judith, this time at the beach with her mother was imprinted on her mind and has become one of her fondest memories of being at the beach. As she told me, "I remember those times even more fondly than being at the beach in the summer."

Think about the wonderful offerings nature provides in your area year-round. Don't you want your children to experience these simple pleasures? What about trekking into the woods to cut down a fresh Christmas tree? Growing pumpkins in a garden of your own making? Heading up to the slopes to ski? Making snow angels? Searching for tadpoles in local rivers? Exploring tide pools? Identifying songbirds in the trees? Stomping through puddles in the rain? Jumping into piles of leaves in the fall? Picking wildflowers in the meadow in the spring? Chasing fireflies in the warm summer evening? Taking a boat trip to watch gray whales migrate from the north? Going fishing at a nearby lake or, perhaps, deep-sea fishing? Riding bikes into the hills and stopping for a picnic lunch?

Remember, nature provides infinite possibilities and an opportunity to see and experience those things that may not be part of our everyday existence. To me, being out in nature is one of the best ways to create a well-rounded and balanced child. Get them out in nature, and let Mother Nature do the rest.

Find Nature Where You Are

Certainly, as a parent, I understand that it is not always possible to get miles away from the city whenever we want. The fact is, our schedules are too full, our lives too crowded with obligations. However, it is important for children (and for us) to keep nature on our list. I once heard someone say that in America if someone wants to find a place to sit down, he or she will have to go to Europe. There's some truth to these words. Here in the States, we have not designed our cities to be inclusive of nature. Land has been viewed as a commodity that is wasted if not developed. Luckily, most neighborhoods and inner-city parks manage to hold their own amidst encroaching urban sprawl. Find a park in your area where your children can go wild, and let the sun shine on their faces. Take evening walks in the chilly air. Create a yard that is inviting to play in. Drive ten to fifteen minutes to a wilderness area where the whole family can take a nature walk. It's amazing. Even here in California, where million-dollar homes are but five feet away from each other, we can get in the car and within fifteen minutes be in a lovely wilderness area where we have seen rattlesnakes, bobcats, hawks, falcons, and colorful lizards.

Nature helps our children to connect—with themselves, with others, and with a higher source. And, like all of us, when they feel connected, they feel balanced. They live the questions and discover that they don't have to have all the right answers. As Buddha once said, "If you wish to know the Divine, feel the wind on your face and the warm sun on your hand."

Resources

Transformative Getaways, by John Benson. New York: Henry Holt, 1996.

Spiritual Literacy: Reading the Sacred in Everyday Life, by Frederic and Mary Ann Brussat. New York: Simon & Schuster Touchstone Book, 1996.

Artists' and Writers' Colonies, by Gail Bowler. Hillsboro, Oreg.: Blue Heron, 1995.

Vacations That Can Change Your Life, by Ellen Lederman. Naperville, Ill.: Source Books, 1996.

Omega Institute (family program), 260 Lake Drive, Rhinebeck, NY 12572-3212; (914) 266-4444; www.omega-inst.org.

Look for nature programs and summer camps in your area offered through community centers, science organizations, public schools, and local clubs.

7

The Importance of
Healthy Living

Americans are overfed and undernourished. Obesity in children is at an all-time high. As a country we spend millions of dollars on weight-loss programs and yet fail to eat balanced diets. Fortunately, many of us are making the necessary changes to improve our children's health through better eating habits. And it's a good thing, too, because candy, fast-food, and overly processed foods are incredibly convenient and easy for our children to become reliant on for standard fare.

Good nutrition is one of the pillars of health. However, simply "eating right" is no longer sufficient. With an over-reliance on processed foods and soil depletion (the soil is not as rich in minerals as it once was) causing the foods in our supermarkets to be less nutritious than in the past, we must make more-conscious, healthful choices about the meals we prepare. No longer a passing fad, the importance of diet for maintaining a balanced physiology, for physical as well as mental well-being, has become a quality-of-life and longevity issue, not only for us, but for our children as well. Science is finding that diet has a profound effect on mood disorders, headaches, sinus problems, allergies, hormonal imbalances, blood sugar, ear infections, anxiety, depression, and other physical and emotional ailments. Certainly, as parents, we want to provide nutritious meals and promote healthy eating habits. Yet we may not always know where to begin when it comes to making the transition from our dependence on prepackaged foods to fresher and alive ingredients. Besides, when we think of healthy diets, many of us find visions of tofu and granola dancing in our heads—not always an appealing incentive to move toward sound nutrition. But do not despair. There are many simple ways to improve your family's nutrition by making incremental and enjoyable changes that everyone can be happy with.

Seven Rules of Thumb for Balanced Eating

1. Reduce sugar consumption. Refined sugars such as sucrose, glucose, corn syrup, and lactose are often used as fillers and additives in foods. They heighten the sweetness of the food product while, simultaneously, heightening blood-sugar levels. The result is elevated energy or hyperactivity, especially in children. Not only is sugar full of empty calories, it also acts to deplete the body of essential B vitamins, which are required for sugar's digestion. Furthermore, one tablespoon of sugar in a sitting reduces white blood cell activity within thirty minutes of ingestion. And white blood cells are essential for proper functioning of the immune system. It is not surprising that children love the taste. However, think about the health consequences and direct them toward more nutritious, naturally sweet foods such as fruit and cheese, yogurt shakes made with chocolate protein powder, or baked goods with fruit and protein powder added into the batter. Keep in mind: if your

child craves and sneaks sugar, he could be suffering from mineral deficiencies. I will discuss this later in this chapter under ADD/ADHD.

2. Restrict the amount of dairy products. The majority of people in the world cannot properly digest cow's milk. Be that as it may, most Americans have numerous servings of dairy products throughout each day: milk on cereal, cheese on our sandwiches, milkshakes, yogurt, and then more cheese in our sauces or milk-based soups. Not only can this increase our fat consumption, but it can also create digestive problems, sinus problems (caused by an overproduction of mucus), and allergic reactions: acne, rashes, postnasal drip, and congestion in the lungs. Don't get me wrong. I love dairy products—ice cream, yogurt, cheese, and milk—but in moderation. Use substitutes occasionally such as soy, rice, or almond milk; soy cheese or sorbet instead of ice cream. Be creative with milkshakes. Add fresh strawberries or fresh peaches to a small amount of vanilla yogurt and ice. Blend and drink. If your child is not susceptible to hyperactivity and is over one year old, add a half a teaspoon of honey. Also, you might look for soy-based ice-cream substitutes, which are tasty!

3. Limit the consumption of processed foods. In our fast-paced lives, it is easy to become reliant upon frozen dinners, pizzas, macaroni and cheese, chips and dip, cheese and crackers prepackaged snacks, and canned soups. Although it is fine to serve these on occasion, especially when you're in a pinch, do your best to provide fresh, organic meats, vegetables, and fruits.

4. Eat quality foods. Eat live foods. Raw spinach; raw carrots; fresh, organic cherries, watermelon, peaches, and strawberries; leafy greens such as kale, collard greens, and lettuce; mushrooms; broccoli; green beans; squash; pumpkin; onions; zucchini; corn on the cob; avocados; the list is endless. Find a grocery store that carries organic products (they are grown without pesticides and chemicals, often in soil that has been composted and, as a result, contains more nutrients for the foods to absorb). Or request that your regular market carry organic produce if they don't already. They usually will oblige. Look for an organic, local farmer's market. Find a delivery service on the World Wide Web. The nutritional value of organic foods is much greater, and you won't be exposing your children to toxic chemicals. Moreover, your children will get more and need to eat less.

5. Drink clean water. Unfortunately, most of our drinking water in the United States today contains an abundance of chlorine and other chemicals used to purify the water—and the sad part is that, even with these chemicals, the water is questionable at best. Purchase purified water from a reputable company or buy water from a known source: Calistoga mineral water, Evian, Perrier, Black Mountain, and so forth. The closer the springs are to where you live, the lower the cost.

6. Use proper food combinations. A good rule of thumb is this: protein and vegetables first, then dairy and carbohydrates. If your child wants a fruit salad, offer a small amount of cheese to go with it. This will balance out the fructose or fruit sugar and carbohydrates by adding

some essential fat to your child's diet. Add protein powder to pancake batter to balance the carbohydrate and fat. Whenever possible, avoid mixing fruits and vegetables—with the exception of apples and pineapples—as they digest differently and fermentation can occur. Try to balance out protein, carbohydrates, and unsaturated fats because most of us, including children, tend to consume an overabundance of carbohydrates. At the end of the chapter are a variety of books with recipes for combining foods. Use these as a guide (not as a bible) for creating healthy food combinations.

7. Give your child a good vitamin supplement. Make sure it has plenty of B vitamins (to combat stress) and C, D, E, and A vitamins to assist the immune system, help with healthy cell production, and build and strengthen healthy bones and teeth. Minerals such as magnesium (bolsters optimum nerve functioning), potassium (helps regulate blood pressure and prevents fatigue), selenium (an antioxidant that works with vitamin E to protect cell membranes and stimulate the immune response), copper (a necessary mineral for the formation of blood cells and healthy skin and hair), zinc (zinc has a variety of important functions; it boosts immunity functioning; maintains health of hair, skin, joints, and eyes; reduces hormonal depression; and helps to enhance reproductive health), and iron (iron is essential for healthy blood) should be contained in your supplements. I would also recommend the old remedy for whatever ails ya': cod liver oil. It comes in easy-to-swallow capsules your children can swallow. Cod liver oil or a serving of fresh salmon once a week provides important fatty acids necessary for maintaining proper brain chemistry and bal-

ancing insulin. Last, consider adding Green Vibrance Super Food to juice, morning smoothies, or to yogurt (just a touch). It is a green algae superfood that is chock-full of vitamins and minerals. It is also one of the most alive foods your children can eat. The following foods are rich in minerals: bananas, seafood, leafy vegetables, nuts, eggs and egg yolks, fruit, lean meat (organic, free-range meat is best), pumpkin seeds, sunflower seeds, sesame seeds, tuna, salmon, cottage cheese, Swiss and Cheddar cheeses, yogurt, whole cereals, unsaturated vegetable oils (preferably cold pressed), avocados, peanut butter, moderate amounts of fresh butter, potatoes, brewer's yeast, lentils, beans and rice (combined for protein), and organic vegetables.

Nutritious Recipes and Meal Ideas

Now that you know what foods are the best for you and why, why not combine these foods into delicious, nutritious breakfasts and lunches? The following recipes are some of my favorites. Express your individuality, and pamper your family's tastebuds, by experimenting with ingredients and flavors.

Great Start Breakfasts:

Smoothies

Papaya Passion
(Papayas contain digestive enzymes.)
1 papaya

2 ripe bananas

½ cup orange juice

1 tablespoon protein powder

Peel and seed papaya. Mix bananas and juice. Blend. Add protein powder.

Strawberry Mint Cold Snap

1 cup mint leaves, loosely packed

1 cup boiling water

5–6 cups frozen strawberries (or watermelon)

½ cup whole milk

1 tablespoon protein powder

Place mint leaves in a bowl and pour boiling water over them. Cover and steep for 10–15 minutes. Drain leaves and save liquid. Place in the refrigerator to chill. Place strawberries (or frozen watermelon), mint liquid, and milk in blender. Mix on high. Add protein powder to taste.

Caribbean Sea Breeze

1 cup pineapple juice

1 cup coconut milk (fresh or canned)

1 cup orange juice

1½ cups ice

1 cup vanilla yogurt (optional)

1 tablespoon freshly grated nutmeg (garnish)

Fresh coconut (garnish)

Blend all the ingredients together until smooth. Then add fresh nutmeg and coconut, if desired, to the top of the drink.

Kids' Creation

1 cup orange juice

2 cups ice
¼ cup purified water
1 cup vanilla yogurt
½ papaya
1 mango
1 banana
1 cup fresh strawberries
2 tablespoons protein powder

Place all the ingredients in the blender one at a time, then blend on high.

Blueberry Blast

½ cup peach juice (no sugar added)
1 cup vanilla frozen yogurt
1 cup blueberries (fresh)
2 tablespoons plain yogurt
1 tablespoon protein powder

Mix the peach juice with the frozen yogurt. Then add the blueberries, yogurt, and protein powder.

Fabulous Fruit

Fruit Salad

1 cup bananas
1 cup seedless grapes
1 cup watermelon
1 cup cantaloupe
1 cup honeydew melon
1 cup papaya
1 cup strawberries
⅓ cup chopped almonds

Mix fruit together and sprinkle almonds on top to add protein and fat to the high sugar (fructose) content in the fruit.

Fruit Salad Topping

1 cup cream cheese

2 tablespoons boiling water

2 cups strawberry yogurt (sweetened with honey or fruit puree)

Nutmeg or grated orange peel (garnish)

Soften the cream cheese by mixing it with the boiling water. Then add yogurt. Top with nutmeg or grated orange peel.

Banana Pancakes

2 cups bananas

Add to your favorite pancake mix (the ones at the health-food store contain less sugar and additives). Then cook in the skillet. Top with a small amount of maple syrup (the real thing)

Apple Pancakes

2 tart green apples

10 tablespoons of unbleached flour

3 teaspoons of granulated fructose

Pinch of salt

4 eggs

1 cup milk

2 tablespoons butter

Cinnamon

Peel and slice apples. Mix dry ingredients together. In a separate bowl, mix eggs and milk. Combine eggs and milk with dry ingredients. Melt 2 tablespoons butter in skillet. Sauté apples until soft. Pour in half of batter and cook until golden brown underneath. Sprinkle the top with cinnamon. Then put the lid on and cook on low heat until pancake is cooked all the way through.

Cottage Cheese Fruit Medley with Raspberry Sauce

1 cup low-fat cottage cheese

¼ cup fresh blueberries

¼ cup sliced peaches

½ cup cantaloupe, diced

½ cup grapes

1½ cups fresh raspberries

6 macadamia nuts *or* 8 almonds

Place cottage cheese in the center of the plate. Arrange fruit (except raspberries) around the cheese. Puree raspberries in the blender, then pour puree over the fruit and cottage cheese. Sprinkle your choice of nuts on top.

Protein Power Breakfasts

Speckled Scrambled Eggs

⅓ cup finely chopped onion

⅓ cup finely chopped carrots

⅓ cup finely chopped broccoli spears

½ tablespoon garlic salt

½ tablespoon parsley flakes (dried or fresh)

¼ tablespoon rosemary

4 eggs

Sauté vegetables with spices until cooked, leaving them a little crunchy. Add eggs and scramble mixture all together.

Turkey Bacon Wrap-a-Round

Olive oil

12 slices of turkey bacon (or finely cut turkey breast)

12 eggs (free-range, cage-free, if possible)

1 cup grated Cheddar cheese

Garlic salt, pepper, paprika, and rosemary

Oil each cup of a muffin tin with olive oil. Line each cup with a strip of precooked bacon or turkey breast. (Turkey bacon often works best if cooked in a microwave oven.) Preheat oven to 350°F. Place an egg in each of the muffin cups. Sprinkle the top with cheese and spices (add a spinach leaf, if desired); then place in the oven until eggs are poached.

Tofu Circles

1 block firm tofu
Olive oil
1 cup fresh spinach
½ cup mushrooms
½ cup onions
Butter
Garlic salt (or fresh garlic, if preferred)
8 English muffin halves
8 very thin Havarti dill cheese slices

Slice the block of tofu (approximately 8 ½-inch-thick slices) and sauté in olive oil until golden brown. Set aside. Lightly steam spinach. Sauté mushrooms and onions in fresh butter. Then add spinach. Sprinkle with garlic salt or add fresh garlic to taste. Toast English muffin halves. When finished, place vegetables on English muffins, then tofu on top of veggies, then place Havarti on top and melt in oven or microwave.

Nutritious Lunches

Tasty Tea

Brew herbal tea (peppermint, spearmint, iced tea herbal blends) and add apple juice to sweeten. This drink is much more cleansing and not as sugary as convenient lunch box drinks.

Good Combinations: Protein
Strips of fresh chicken on sticks *or* small chicken legs (3–4)
    (glaze with soy sauce, steak sauce, or teriyaki sauce)
Turkey jerky
Peanut butter sandwich with no-sugar jelly
Tofu squares (sautéed with soy sauce)
Tuna sandwich
Salmon steaks or strips
Chicken cubes to place on crackers

Good Combinations: Vegetables
Raw carrot sticks
Chilled asparagus
Broccoli with dip
Crunchy green beans with almonds
Celery with peanut butter
Red potatoes (halved and seasoned)
Fresh salsa (with chips)

Good Combinations: Fruit
Apples, applesauce
Bananas
Fruit salad
Peaches, strawberries
Cherries, plums, oranges
Avocados

Good Combinations: Fat
Cheese (string, Cheddar, etc.)

Peanut butter
Nuts and seeds

Try choosing one item from two of these good-combination categories and putting them together for your children's lunches. Occasional chips and crackers are fine, but try to give them fresh, healthy (protein- and vitamin-filled foods) in balanced combinations such as those listed above instead of empty calories. Diet is the foundation for health as well as a preventive measure for avoiding problems such as "pica": a severe, obsessive craving for sugary and salty foods that results from lack of minerals.

Attention Deficit Disorder (ADD) and Attention Deficit Hyperactivity Disorder (ADHD)

Natural Way magazine quotes Gerald Olarsch, N D , as linking violent behavior, hyperactivity, and learning disabilities to a fundamental lack of minerals. In the article, authors Nina Andersen and Howard Peiper point out that mineral deficiencies translate into a variety of behaviors ranging from excessive fatigue and a sluggish mental response, to hyperactivity, aggression, and hyperexcitability. The following minerals are listed in relation to Attention Deficit Disorder (ADD) and Attention Deficit Hyperactivity Disorder (ADHD):

- Dimethylglycine (DMG): DMG is found in trace amounts in some foods such as rice hulls. When it was administered to autistic children, parents reported improved behavior and speech as well as an increase in the frustration threshold, all within twenty-four hours. There is also evidence that DMG may improve the effectiveness of other nutrients, such as B_6 and magnesium.

- Magnesium: Low levels of magnesium are associated with states of hyperexcitability and distractability. Unfortunately, most children do not receive sufficient amounts of this important mineral in their diets.

- Essential fatty acids: Commonly recommended for PMS and related symptoms, borage oil, primrose oil, and flaxseed oil are some of the best sources for essential fatty acids. Flax meal is another option as it can be sprinkled on cereal, yogurt, or cottage cheese. Research has shown that those children who are not deficient in essential fatty acids learn faster and seem to have better brain functioning overall (another reason essential fatty acids are so important in the case of ADD).

- Zinc: Zinc must be carefully administered according to a child's size and weight. For this reason, you may wish to consult a naturopathic nutritionist, as this is his or her specialty. Dr. Estaban Genoa has had great success treating ADD children with supplements of liquid electrolyte trace minerals and zinc.

- Enzymes: Enzymes are essential for proper digestion. However, our bodies do not produce all the enzymes needed to sustain healthy digestion (and healthy digestion is required for the absorption of the nutrients found in the foods we eat). The other enzymes must come from foods—and only *raw* foods contain enzymes. Cooked and processed foods do not supply the body with needed enzymes. For this reason, we must eat foods such as raw vegetables and fruits (especially papaya). Otherwise, enzyme deficiency can create symptoms such as chronic irritability and fatigue, digestive upset, impaired mental capacity, and food allergies. Studies have shown that food allergies are linked to extreme behaviors as well as mood disorders.

- Allergies: Recently, a revolutionary technique for diagnosing and treating food allergies has come to the forefront of complementary medicine. Complementary medicine includes preventive and alternative treatment—anything that can be used in conjunction with traditional Western medicine. It is called the Nambudripad Allergy Elimination Technique, or NAET. NAET involves muscle testing (a method often familiar to chiropractors) and a simple fifteen-minute acupressure treatment to relieve allergic reactions to common foods, chemicals, plants, animal dander, and other substances that are offensive to a large number of people. For children diagnosed with ADD or ADHD, NAET can be helpful in eliminating the irritation of allergies, thereby calming the system and, it is hoped, any behaviors associated with it. For information on how to find a practitioner, call (800) 842-3636 and ask for Dr. Ellen Cutler's book, *Winning the War Against Asthma and Allergies*, for $13.95. Dr. Cutler's book includes a listing of 200 practitioners and a website: www.naet.com.

If your child has been diagnosed with ADD or ADHD you might try consulting complementary medical experts such as naturopaths (nutrition), homeopaths (alternative prescriptions), and those involved with relaxation techniques. It is quite possible that you would see marked improvements in your child's quality of life even if you decided to continue with medication.

Alternatives to Antibiotics

Antibiotics have saved my life. They are powerful and useful drugs that are often prescribed in the United States for infections and other ailments—and they are effective but not selective. Antibiotics work to rid our bodies of those germs that attack our system, yet they simultaneously go after our system's own defense mechanisms, sometimes causing an unpleasant side effect: diarrhea. If we use antibiotics often, they lose their effectiveness. Knowing this, why do physicians often prescribe antibiotics in cases where they are not very useful? Even in instances when they may be detrimental to our health? The answer is this: convenience. Fortunately, there are alternatives that are equally convenient in treating infections, flus, and colds—and they have a preventive component that can help strengthen our children's systems against future illnesses. Here are some of the alternatives:

- Echinacea and goldenseal: Both are natural herbal remedies. They come in liquid form and can be added to juice, tea, or purified water or given directly out of the bottle. Special formulas designed specifically for children are available at most health-food stores.
- Homeopathic medicines: Various homeopathic remedies are considered highly effective against ear infections, flus, fevers, and a variety of colds. Among them are aconite, belladonna, calcarea carbonica, pulsatilla, and sulphur. Mercurius is also very useful

for strep throat (an illness that is commonly treated with antibiotics). If your child has recurring symptoms, I strongly suggest that you contact a homeopath in your area before your child develops a resistance to more traditional drug therapies.

Resources for Homeopathy

International Foundation for Homeopathy
P.O. Box 7
Edmonds, WA 98020-0007
(206) 776-4147 or (206) 776-1499 (fax)

Homeopathic Academy of Naturopathic Physicians
P.O. Box 69565
Portland, OR 97201
(503) 761-3298 or (503) 762-1929 (fax)

The National Center for Homeopathy
801 North Fairfax #306
Alexandria, VA 22314
(703) 548-7790 or (703) 548-7792 (fax)

Exercise

Involving children in a regular exercise routine, especially one that is fun, can contribute to a lifelong relationship with exercise that has immeasurable benefits. Consider these facts:

- Unwanted pregnancy is 33 percent less likely to occur in young women who exercise regularly.
- Exercise works as an antidepressant and can be the body's best defense against nervous exhaustion.
- Exercise is fun, and it makes you feel good!

- Playful exercise done together, as a family, can create a more cohesive family life.
- Exercise helps children and adults feel more confident in their bodies.
- Exercise, done without pressure, can create a positive body image, thereby reducing the chances of eating disorders.
- Exercise aids in digestion as well as strengthens muscles and increases endurance.
- Exercise doesn't have to be strenuous to be good for you. Taking walks and going for scenic strolls are beneficial to heart, legs, and lungs.
- Exercise helps children to release their abundant energy in a positive and directed way.
- Exercise soothes anxiety and tension. It helps children and adults to sleep better.
- Exercise improves coordination and balance.
- Exercise is a wonderful way to get you and your children out of the house and into the fresh air and sunshine (or, depending on where you live, the cold, invigorating air).
- Exercise out in nature away from the city's excessive stimulation. You and your children's attitudes will improve.
- Hike in the woods or in the mountains. This will help your children to appreciate the outdoors.
- Take vacations that involve outdoor exercise. Go on adventures out in nature instead of spending the entire holiday within the confines of a hotel and its grounds.
- Swim, snorkle, run, walk, and play ball tag, catch, tag, and chase. Roll in the grass, boat in the lake, ice skate, roller skate, and go fishing, bike riding,

rowing, sledding, and snowball fighting. Go to the gym, to the recreation center, to the park, to the skating rink, to the sprinklers, to the neighbor's pool, to the river, to the woods, to the mountains, and to the valleys and hills. Ride a horse; ride a bike; do gymnastics, karate, tai chi, aerobics; play soccer, basketball, baseball, hockey, jump rope, hopscotch, four square, touch football; go jogging, lifting, and golfing . . . Just exercise! You will all feel better.

Creating a Clean Home Environment

Lead paint. Toxic fumes. Dyes and chemicals that irritate the skin and cause allergies. Poorly circulated air. Unpurified water. Dust, dander, pollen, and mold. These and many other household pollutants can compromise your family's health. Fortunately, many improvements can be made simply by changing detergents, filtering the air and water, replacing bedding, and bringing more light into your home. Consider this:

- **Laundry disks**: Ceramic laundry disks are available for chemically sensitive people. The metallic elements in the activated ceramics produce ionized oxygen, which breaks up dirt and organic compounds, cleaning your family's clothes without harsh detergents. They can be ordered from Real Goods, (800) 762-7325 or (707) 468-9214.
- **Vegetable-based cleansers**: Natural cleaning products for the house are made with vegetable-based cleaning agents and essential oils. They are biodegradable and are not tested on animals. Unlike popular brands, they do not contain chemical

ingredients. Contact Environmentally Sound Products, Life Tree Cleanser (800) 886-5432.

- **Healthy pillows**: All-cotton pillows seem to be immensely helpful for those who are irritated by down or synthetic fiberfill. If your child is frequently congested or has difficulty sleeping, you might consider a new pillow. KB makes pillows without bleach or dyes. Contact KB Cotton Pillows (800) 544-3752.
- **Air purification**: There are a variety of air-filter products currently on the market. They range in price and size. You may want to look into the products available. Mia Rose Products offers air purifiers at (800) 292-6339.

Resources for a Nontoxic Home

Many resources are available to assist families interested in creating a healthier nontoxic home. I recommend the following organizations:

Household Hazardous Waste Project
P.O. Box 108
Springfield, MO 65804
(417) 836-5777
Publishes *Guide to Hazardous Products Around the Home*

Inform
120 Wall Street, 16th Floor
New York, NY 10005-4001
(212) 361-2400
Publishes *Tackling Toxics in Everyday Products*

CO-OP America
1612 K Street NW, Suite 600
Washington, DC 20006
Members receive a directory of environmentally sound products.

Books

The Natural House Catalogue, by David Pearson. New York: Fireside Book, Simon & Schuster, 1996.

The Healthy House: How to Buy One How to Build One How to Cure a Sick One, by John Bower. Bloominton, Ind.: Healthy House Institute, 1989.

Healing Environments: Your Guide to Indoor Well-Being, by Carol Venolia and Deborah Lynn Dadd. Berkeley, Calif.: Celestial Arts, 1988.

Sustaining the Earth: Choosing Consumer Products That Are Safe for You, Your Family, and the Earth, by Debra Dadd-Redalia. New York: Hearst, 1994.

Resources for Health

Mastering the Zone, by Barry Sears, Ph.D. New York: HarperCollins, 1997.

Zone Perfect Meals in Minutes, by Barry Sears, Ph.D. New York: HarperCollins, 1997.

Natural Prozac, by Joel Robertson, M.D., with Tom Monte. San Francisco: HarperCollins, 1997.

Potatoes Not Prozac, by Kathleen DesMaisons, Ph.D. New York: Simon & Schuster, 1998.

What Are We Feeding Our Kids? by Michael F. Jacobson, Ph.D. New York: Workman Publishing, 1994.

Goddess in the Kitchen, by Margie Lapanja. Berkeley, Calif.: Conari Press, 1998.

The Mayo Clinic Williams Sonoma Cookbook: Simple Solutions for Eating Well, by John Phillip Carroll. San Francisco, Calif.: Time-Life Books, 1998.

Natural Health magazine
P.O. Box 7442
Red Oak, IA 51591-2442

Natural Remedies magazine
P.O. Box 420724
Palm Coast, FL 32142-8671

Natural Way magazine
P.O. Box 52170
Boulder, CO 80322-2170

8

Mentors and Guides

Living in the fast-paced, transient population of the Bay Area of California, I am all too aware of the effort it takes to create and maintain a sense of community. Families are always coming and going, transferred into the area for the computer industry or transferred out of the area because the start-up company they had set their hopes on failed; and it is too expensive to live here without a fairly substantial income.

Many families are too busy to build friendships because both parents are working simply to make ends meet. Separated from relatives, they have to rely solely on each other, and this leaves little time for socializing and becoming a familiar face in the neighborhood. As I wrote in one of my previous books, *Restoring Balance to a Mother's Busy Life*:

> Systems of support formerly provided by the community no longer exist . . . What is the result? Mothers tend to question themselves, wondering what they are doing wrong and why they cannot keep up with the enormous demands, not realizing that over the years the community has fallen away, leaving more and more gaps to be filled by mothers. It is no wonder mothers are often overtaxed and overburdened, and yet they strive to keep

up, responding to images of Superwoman instead of learning to take care of themselves in meaningful ways.

Certainly, this phenomenon is no longer solely the domain of mothers. Both parents are feeling the pressure. While the Bay Area may be an extreme example, it is not so different for many families all across the United States right now. Under circumstances such as these, it is not surprising that mentors and guides are seemingly difficult, if not impossible, to find. But don't lose hope; they *are* there, and they are very important to our children's well-being and sense of self.

The Importance of Mentors

In a sense, mentors complete the circle that cannot be drawn together by two parents (or even one). And this feeling of being surrounded by support creates balance in our children's lives. What we don't or can't provide, our children can get from others. Or they can get more (love, affection, education, wisdom, fun, corny jokes, perspectives on world affairs, and so forth) from those they trust besides their parents. Rather than expecting all their needs and wants to be fulfilled by their parents, children can learn to receive from others; they can learn different lifestyles from others; how to succeed from others; and ways to meet their own needs from the suggestions and teachings of mentors and guides.

As most indigenous people know, the fabric of a society is held together by its ability to live in strong and sustainable communities whereby the needs of an individual are equal to the needs of the group. A civilization in decline, however, does not respect the need for cohesion, mutual trust, and responsibility to others and, instead, begins to look and act more like each man out for himself. Indigenous people know the value of social support systems, especially concerning the raising of children. It does "take a village," because just as two people joined by marriage and commitment cannot fulfill each other's every need, so, too, do our children need others around them who will teach them, serve them, and help them to grow in meaningful ways. In the words of author John Welwood in his book *Love and Awakening,* "Someone who loves us can often see our soul potential more clearly than we can ourselves. When this happens, it has a catalytic effect, it invites and encourages the dormant, undeveloped part to come forth and find expression." This is one of the main purposes of finding mentors and guides for our children— and following our children's lead when they come upon someone who can fulfill a special role in their lives.

Mentors and guides can come from anywhere. They can be teachers, relatives, friends, older or younger children, animals, therapists, school counselors, janitors, local grocers, priests, rabbis, ministers, coaches, karate instructors, neighbors, grandparents, someone else's grandparents, a Big Brother or Sister, a carpenter, a day-care provider, or anyone who takes a sincere interest in our children and is openly willing to invite them into their lives. Never underestimate the impact one person can have.

When I was growing up, my parents were divorced while I was in elementary school. Like most children, I felt more sorrow than I thought I could bear. I lost confidence in myself, thinking that, somehow, I must be to blame. Then, in third grade, I had a wonderful teacher named Peggy Reichtman. I will never forget her gentle face, nor will I forget her dangling earrings and the words she said to me in the spring of the year. "I'm sending your poetry home to your parents for them to see," she told me. "You are gifted, and I hope you will pursue your talents." Such big words, but as an eight-year-old, I knew exactly what she meant. I carried those poems home, bursting with pride and excitement in my heart. As if that wasn't enough, Mrs. Reichtman, who happened to live in our neighborhood, stopped by the house when my mother returned from work, and I heard her tell my mother about my poems. Although nothing formal ever came of it, my mother eventually placed me in an alternative school that emphasized the creative arts. It was there that I began to excel in creative writing, literature, and photography as well as math, science, social studies, civics, and the humanities. I continued to have exceptional teachers who not only taught me about the curriculum, but about my talents and life itself.

In ninth grade, I returned to a public school when I moved in with my father. Fortunately, half my classes were in the Alternative Learning Program designed for self-motivated students. One of my biggest challenges was learning to write an essay for my English class—the same class where I had been asked to put away Erica Jong's *Fear of Flying* because the provocative picture on the cover was "too mature," as Mrs. Moses so delicately phrased it, for the other students. Besides, it was disruptive. Anyway, my teacher, one of my classmates, and my father all tried, unsuccessfully, to explain to me what an essay was. The concept was too foreign. After two days, I still didn't get it. Finally, with my father's unwaivering persistence, I understood and I wrote my first essay. Today, I'm a writer. When people ask me if it takes discipline, I always tell them "Yes, but not like you think." The truth is, I cannot not write. I am compelled. It is part of me, like it was for my mother and my poet grandmother before me.

I do not share this story to toot my own horn. Rather, it is to reassure parents that our children's truest passions will stick with them regardless of whether we enroll them in classes and actively pursue each talent they demonstrate. As Myla and Jon Kabat-Zinn (authors of *Everyday Blessings*) attest, "Many people credit one special person, who gave them soul recognition and encouragement to be who they were, as the source of their success in their life. The mentoring of children and adolescents by people who themselves know in some way their own wholeness, and can thus give selflessly to bring out the beauty and wholeness in others, is the sacred responsibility of the adults in any healthy society." Take notice when one of these people crosses your child's path.

Finding Mentors for Our Children

Not so long ago, when neighborhoods were safe and children could wander from door to door, hanging out with one family, having dinner with another, calling their folks to "check in," mentors and guides were available in abundance. While I was growing up in St. Louis, the rich diversity of our community offered me a variety of mentors and guides, wise men and women who, by sharing their life stories with me, gave me incredible insights and understanding. Jewish grandmothers who spoke to me of the Holocaust; boisterous Italian families who all spoke at the same time and squeezed me until I couldn't breathe; black women who taught me about strength and songs and how to stand up for myself; Irish Catholics whose lively humor helped me to see when not to take life so seriously. I was welcomed into all of their homes. The wisdom I learned, the joy and warmth I experienced being privy to their lives and having them be genuinely interested in mine, ignited my imagination and enlivened my spirit simply because they had time for me. They were interested in what I had to say. They marveled at my "deep thoughts." They smiled at my silly mistakes, and they comforted me through my disappointments. They were some of my greatest teachers.

Unfortunately, many neighborhoods have changed, and, as parents, we are responsible for seeking those individuals who want to be a part of our children's lives. Just because we have to look beyond our own backyards, however, doesn't necessarily mean we have to look far. Be on the lookout for special, trustworthy people who seem to appear on the scene: a new teacher's assistant whose exotic tales of her travels enchant the children; a friendly gardener who talks to the plants and encourages the children to learn how to tend to a garden; a school janitor who stops pushing his broom to catch up on the children's daily news; an elderly person who lives down the street; a special guest who brings his computer knowledge to the community center; a music instructor who runs a small music school where all the students seems to have a wonderful time learning to sing or play an instrument. The list is endless.

The following are suggestions for what to look for when searching for individuals who will be more than simply a teacher or instructor and instead will be a life guide for our children.

1. Be selective. Feel free to interview schoolteachers to find out how long they have been teaching. Do they still genuinely love their job or are they burned out? Do they listen and fully engage with students or do they simply like to lecture? Do they take a wide range of student interests into account or do they only stick to the lesson?

2. Choose an instructor. When choosing an instructor for an art, gymnastics, ice skating, or reading class, or any other class at your local community center, art studio, or elsewhere, be sure to visit the facility ahead of time. If possible, observe how a class is taught before signing up. Do you like the way the instructor handles the children? Does he listen? Is he respectful of shy and slow-to-warm children, or does he just thrust everyone into the activities? Is he as eager to listen to girls as he is to boys? Does he take pride in the activity? Does he cultivate a sense of fun and enjoyment for the children? Is he authoritarian and demanding? If so, will this fit with your children's temperaments or will it turn them away from their love of music, art, sports, or reading?

   • Will the instructor use the activity to teach optimism and to develop confidence and character? Or will he stick only to the task at hand, focusing more readily on the end result?

   • Will the instructor overpower the children in attendance or challenge them in meaningful ways?

   • Is the instructor open to parental involvement or does he act as though the class is only his domain?

   • Is the instructor enthusiastic? Does he have a love of the sport, art, game? Does his personality complement our children's?

3. Nurture the mentor relationship. When children start to speak highly of someone we may not be aware of—a serendipitous meeting at school, in the neighborhood, in a class, and so forth—it is important that we meet this new person and help to make our children accessible to him or her. It may mean extra driving, having them

over to dinner, or meeting at the local pool. But it is important to nurture the relationship, especially if there is no doubt that the relationship is a positive one. Give them the gift of time together.

4. Encourage community involvement. As I said earlier, community is very important. It provides our children with many other adults, teens, and children who can offer them things we cannot. Like the indigenous people who do not feel threatened if a son or a daughter spends lots of time with an elder or another member of the tribe (in fact, some children may move in with a mentor for a time), it is important that we, as parents, respect and honor what others who are different from us can contribute to our children's lives. We may not always be comfortable with our children's sovereignty. What they share with others may highlight what is different and unique about our children. We may discover that our children have very different interests than we do. They may not share our deep love of music and art. They may never learn ballet or computers or any of the things we cherish, things that may be part of our identity. Good mentors will not take our children away from us. Rather, they will make their contribution to our children, just as we do. Our children will be richer for it.

5. Trust your intuition. You know your children better than anyone else. If you truly respect who your children are, in their own right, then you will know what to offer them, when. And you will know when they need

something you might not be able to give them. But your support in finding someone who can offer them something you can't will never be forgotten. Your children will know you love and respect them, as individuals. And that you are mature enough to let them grow beyond your limitations, beyond your comfort zone, and in directions that may differ from your own. In the wise words of James Keller; "A candle loses nothing of its light by lighting another candle."

Resources

Restoring Balance to a Mother's Busy Life, by Beth Wilson Saavedra, Chicago: NTC/Contemporary Books, 1996.

The Mentor Spirit: Life Lessons on Leadership and the Art of Encouragment, by Marsha Sinetar. New York: St. Martin's, 1998.

The Wonder of Boys: What Parents, Mentors and Educators Can Do to Shape Boys into Extraordinary Men, by Michael Gurian. New York: Putnam, 1996.

It Takes a Village, by Hillary Rodham Clinton. New York: Simon & Schuster, 1996.

Mothers as Mentors: Workshops for Mothers and Daughters, by Jennifer Louden. Write to: P.O. Box 3584, Santa Barbara, CA 93130; or go to the website: www .loudenbooks.com.

Love and Awakening: Discovering the Sacred Path of Intimate Relationship, by John Welwood. New York: Harper-Collins, 1996.

Everyday Blessings, by Myla Kabat-Zinn and Jon Kabat-Zinn. New York: Hyperion, 1998.

9

Building Character and Optimism

Depression among children is steadily rising. Teens feel lost. The old order is failing, and we don't always know what to replace it with. "Generation X" (those born between the years 1966 and 1980) is the first generation in our 200-year history not expected to meet, or exceed, their parents' financial success. Even those of us born in the final years of the baby boom are experiencing the end of the American dream, not only in financial terms, but in spiritual, emotional, and psychological ones as well. Cynicism and pessimism are infecting our children's attitude toward life. And while it may be easy to dismiss this outlook as simply a passing phase, it is not. Dr. Martin E. P. Seligman writes in his book *The Optimistic Child*, "Pessimism is an entrenched habit of mind that has sweeping and disastrous consequences: depressed mood, resignation, underachievement, and even unexpectedly poor physical health. Pessimism is not shaken in the natural course of life's ups and downs. Rather, it hardens with each setback and soon becomes self-fulfilling. America is in the midst of an epidemic of pessimism and is suffering from its most serious consequence, depression."

Without a doubt, we are a society in transition. The paradigms that once governed successfully have outlived

their usefulness. The situation in which we now find ourselves is both a frightening and exciting one because,
although many changes may feel bigger than life and out of
our control, we do have choices. Our children have choices.
And just knowing that choices exist creates hope—and hope
is the greatest enemy of depression. It is the opposite of
depression. It is optimism.

Having an inner sense of optimism is essential for balance in our children. Otherwise, it is too easy for them to
succumb to what is cool. And, currently, negative is cool;
ignorance is cool; being a maverick is cool; making money,
not necessarily friends, is cool; acting like you already know
everything is cool. Being excited about life, love, and learning is, at least attitudinally, uncool, even nerdish. Balancing
out the prevailing attitudes of pop culture provides our children with positive options so they can more joyfully navigate the difficulties that will inevitably cross their paths.
They can maintain their optimism and love of life despite
external pressures and the hard knocks. As author Thomas
Moore writes in his book *The Re-Enchantment of Everyday
Life*, "During my years as a psychotherapist, I felt that people bringing me their stories of a foundering career, a failing
marriage, a tenacious depression, or an overpowering addiction were suffering from a deeper malaise. They had fallen
out of love with life itself." But as Moore can attest, there
are those who, regardless of many hardships, manage to
avoid modern despair because they love themselves and their
lives. He goes on to say, "If we imagine paradise deeply
enough, we won't be literally childish or naive, but we can
live with a positive life amid many kinds of torment."
Teaching our children to take the higher road will serve
them immeasurably in the years to come.

Optimism and Virtue

Building optimism and personal power in our children is more important today than ever. Our children are bombarded with television programs and films that undermine family unity. They portray adults as overbearing simpletons who are not worth listening to and, in subtle and not-so-subtle ways, encourage children to be smart mouthed, arrogant, and disrespectful. As psychologist and author Mary Pipher writes in her book *The Shelter of Each Other,* "Our culture is at war with families. Families in America have been invaded by technology, mocked or 'Kitschified' by the media, isolated by demographic changes, pounded by economic forces and hurt by corporate values."

It is no wonder, then, that our children feel conflicted. The values taught at home and those demonstrated in the larger pop culture are often at odds with each other. For this reason, it is essential that we, as parents, focus our efforts on building optimism and a sound foundation of character. Teaching virtues does not mean forming a rigid set of rules for our children's behavior. Rather, we provide a working set of options whereby our children can make solid choices in a variety of complex and changing situations. When children perceive themselves as having options and the power to make wise and thoughtful choices, they feel strong and optimistic instead of feeling resigned, depressed, and angrily rebellious. In addition, teaching our children the value of virtues such as empathy, courage, respect, honesty, self-reliance, self-reflection, self-love, and so on gives them the opportunity to filter these lessons through their own internal belief systems to find the best ways to apply them to the rapidly changing landscape in which we currently find ourselves. In an article that appeared in the February 1998 publication of the Institute of Noetic Sciences, *Connections*, twenty-three-year-old Matthew Frazer wrote:

> There is a dire need to reintroduce the 'examined life' into our generation. Without it, our very evolutionary progress could exhaust the numinous aspect of our being and create an unprecedented psychic schism. Manifestations of this schism can already be seen. Technological 'advances' that tout increased productivity and infinite communicative possibilities act conversely to mechanize their users. At the same time, alcohol and drugs are being used to numb our natural yearnings for emotional connection and spiritual evolution . . . However, transcending the prominent values and practices is often a desolate experience . . . I suggest a 'look inward' as a start . . . because I am confident that self-reflection will reveal the human commonalities inherent in all of our natures and ultimately call for their cultivation.

In short, teaching virtues builds a resolute character—a strong inner foundation of self-knowledge upon which choices can be made.

Building Character

As parents, our primary responsibility is to teach our children the virtues they need to carry them throughout life. After all, we form the inner circle of their daily lives. Sure, we share our inner circle with caregivers, schoolteachers, close friends, and, if we're lucky, grandparents and other relatives. But the fact remains: we are our children's first link to the outside world; our bond runs deep. Certainly, teaching virtues can seem to be a daunting task, an uphill battle, and a lonely endeavor at times, yet we need not be intimidated. The rewards are great.

In the inspirational words of Mary Botham Howitt: "God sent children for another purpose than merely keeping up the race—to enlarge our hearts; and make us unselfish and full of kindly sympathies and affections; to give our souls higher aims." It is precisely these "higher aims" that must be cultivated in our children so they will emerge as adults with well-rounded, balanced characters. As much as we'd like to believe that our children have good hearts and intelligent minds and can act with empathy and compassion, the truth is we must help them to develop these virtues to fill out their characters.

Three Ways to Create an Environment That Nurtures Higher-Aim Growth

1. The simplest daily activities can be turned into lessons of love that will last. And if you miss a teaching moment the first time around, always remember: other teaching moments will present themselves, often when you least expect them. For example, the next time your child refuses to share an ice cream bar, take a moment to slow the pace of the day and mindfully point out that others will be less inclined to share with him the next time around. Done without guilt-inducing exhortations to be good, your child has a choice to make about sharing, an informed choice that can, eventually, teach him when he wants to include others, and share with others, and when he wants to say, "No, not this time." Seems simple, yet if we, as parents, build on this type of knowledge brick by brick, our children will have the

opportunity to learn some valuable lessons about inner values and the ways in which these values shape our actions in the world.

2. It is not all up to you. Find mentors and guides. Direct your children toward those who have already developed a positive sense of self. But keep in mind who your children are. If you keep introducing introverts to very social, boisterous, and outgoing children with high self-esteem, instead of feeling good about themselves, they may feel as though you want them to be more like their opposite, not themselves. Choose others who bring out the best in your children and cherish their individual temperaments. If your children feel respected for who they are, they are much more likely to listen and take in the wisdom, lessons, and teachings of others.

3. Allow your children to explore beyond the current value structure of your family. Yes, as parents, it is essential that our values be respected. Yet we must also take care not to confine our children to a rigid value system even if it worked for our parents and their parents before them. Our children are unique individuals who may wish to explore more deeply, question authority, and interpret our family values through their own understanding of reality. Besides, the world they are confronting is a very different place. Give support as your children excavate their souls. Explore with them when the opportunities arise. Although this may be a more-demanding approach to parenting, remember: respecting each other's differences will allow you to find common ground more quickly. You can focus on each

other's gifts instead of insisting that you both see the world through exactly the same lens.

Nine Important Virtues and Simple Ways to Teach Them

1. *Empathy*. As discussed in Chapter 3, many of the temperament types listed needed lessons in empathy as well as tolerance and understanding of others' emotions. Although many of us would like to believe that the virtue of empathy is inbred, it is not. Some types excel in it—to the point of codependence. For other types, it is a foreign concept. Certainly not an inner knowledge that they can feel inside their bodies viscerally. If our children have difficulty empathizing, how will they avoid adopting an "everyone is out for themselves" approach to life that seems so prevalent these days? As authors Barbara C. Unell and Dr. Jerry L. Wyckoff write in their book *20 Teachable Virtues*, "Establishing your own personal living standards and living by those standards involves no magic, only the setting of priorities and the active choosing of moral and ethical ways of behaving over the self-centered, what's-in-it-for-me, winning-at-all-costs approach to life that has become the vogue."

- Illustrate empathy by the example of caring words: "I'm sorry you hurt yourself." "Can I carry that for you? It looks too heavy for you." "That must have hurt your feelings when she said that to you."

- Illustrate empathy through the example of caring actions. Show that you recognize and understand the emotions of others: walk over and help your child dust himself off if he falls instead of saying, "Oh, you're fine." Let your child know that you share her feelings by sitting on the floor and holding her in your lap as you discuss her disappointment, sadness, embarrassment, and so forth. "I can see you're disappointed that your friend can't play. I would be disappointed, too."

- Avoid giving punishment in kind. For example, if your child purposefully splashes soap bubbles in another child's eyes, instead of splashing her back to "see how this feels," help her to understand why the other child is in tears. Unell and Wyckoff assert that, "children who experience punishment in kind only increase their anger and aggressiveness, lose respect for the adult who administers it, and reduce their ability to feel empathy."

- Take the opportunity to point out and compliment empathetic behavior: "Wasn't it nice that Sara helped you with your homework? She could tell that you were feeling tired and frustrated with the work, and so she helped you complete it." "I really appreciate it when you wait to ask me to do something after I've just returned home from work. You seem to understand that I'm often tense and worn-out after work and need a little time to unwind before I jump into activities at home. Thanks!"

2. *Courage.* Children need courage to counteract the many negative influences barraging them today. They need to feel comfortable with themselves so they can overcome peer pressure, fear, and doubt. They even need the

courage to admit when they are wrong (some parents aren't even this courageous!).

- Illustrate the example of courage through words: "You can do it!" "You were brave to swim across the lake. Great job!" "No, I do not wish to give a donation, and I would appreciate it if you would not knock on my door." "I don't feel comfortable doing that, why don't we come up with something else?"

- Illustrate courage through the example of actions: if a physician is handling your child roughly, gently but firmly place your hand on the physician's and make it clear with your words and your eyes that she will need to be more considerate of your child. Show your children that you are not afraid to grow and change by admitting fault and finding better ways to express your anger in the future.

- Have the courage to say no to certain TV programs and movies. Have the courage to express your beliefs even if they are unpopular. Be a peaceful warrior. Have the courage to be an advocate for your children. And have the courage to express your love and feelings even if it makes you vulnerable to those closest to you.

3. *Humor.* Humor is the ability to see and appreciate the amusing or comical in a variety of situations. It is also a tool by which we can regain our perspective and see choices that may have eluded us. Laughter is a balm, a squeal of delight, a letting go of tension and throwing away of cares. Finding the humor in life is an important

virtue because it makes us more resilient in the face of adversity and it encourages us to absorb the joy that awaits us, in small and not-so-small ways, everyday.

- Demonstrate the lighter side through humorous words. After dropping a bag of groceries on the floor, ask: "Would you like to see that trick again?!" Laugh at mistakes instead of being angry. "We looked like the three stooges!" we say, recounting a three-legged race at a family picnic. We all get to laugh again.

- Demonstrate humor in your actions. Silly, physical humor is a great source of fun for most families: throw a sponge ball in a weird way; encourage slapstick routines; douse someone in the shower with a cold glass of water. Remember, be playful with children. Play in the pool, on the lawn, in the woods, and on the floor.

- Encourage appropriate humor in your children. Help your children understand the difference between good humor and humor that relies excessively on put-downs. Help them learn when not to laugh at someone else's mishaps even when they seem comical because they might hurt someone's feelings. Decide what your family's rules are for humor that centers around natural body functions. Jokes about pooping and farts are part of the child vernacular. Try not to overreact. Unell and Wyckoff point this out: "Because children naturally use humor to reduce their anxiety about the things that are happening to them, overreacting to any offensive humor will only increase their anxiety and help them feel ashamed of themselves." Finally, don't be afraid to correct your children when they use too much sarcasm and snide remarks to make a point. They may be trying to be humorous, mimicking much of the dialogue that passes as so-called clever humor nowadays, so let them know, kindly but firmly, when it becomes caustic or disrespectful of others' feelings.

- Be careful not to laugh *at* children. They often consider it to be a put-down, and they may feel humiliated and lose their self-respect. When you do find their actions funny, let them know you are enjoying their humor.

4. *Respect.* In the words of the Earl of Chesterfield, "True politeness is a perfect ease in freedom. It simply consists in treating others just as you love to be treated yourself." Respect is such a simple virtue, yet the irony is that one must first respect oneself. But how does a person learn self-respect? By being treated with respect. Thus, to teach our children to be respectful and considerate of the needs and feelings of others, we must model those behaviors to our children, even when our viewpoints differ. Respect means honoring the rights of others and taking them into account in terms of your own actions. It means treating others as you would like to be treated and respecting others' limits, boundaries, and privacy.

- Illustrate respect through the example of your words. Words are very powerful. They can assault one's sense of self, wound or elevate the spirit. Talk to children in a way that demonstrates to them that you respect their feelings and their character. Instead of saying, "You are such a pest!" when angered, deal directly with your child's behavior: "When you ask the same question fifty times, it makes me feel frustrated." Or, if your children spill some milk, don't tell them they are stupid or clumsy. Instead, ask them to help you clean up the mess.

- Illustrate respect through the example of your actions. Do you treat friends in a more-polite and considerate way than other family members? If so, what message does this send? Are you impatient with your children's mistakes yet model tolerance when it is someone else's child? Be consistent. Modeling respect for others when it is also applied to our children helps them to see another's point of view and behaviors that demonstrate caring. Simple actions such as using good manners, asking permission to use something that belongs to someone else before you start to use it, allowing privacy, and taking time to listen and respond to the words of others are worth their weight in gold.

5. *Patience*. The truth is, many of us thought we were patient people until we had kids. Then, we realized we had to take this virtue to a whole new level. What can I say? Children build character! Why is it so important for our children to develop patience? Because patience is the ability to delay wants; hold steady in adverse situations so change can be created; tolerate frustration and difficult challenges so they can be overcome; rein in

impulsive desires so more-thoughtful choices can be made; and understand that one cannot always have everything one wants (immediately!).

- Use patient words. By using encouraging words instead of angry or exasperated ones, we teach our children how to be more patient. Instead of responding to their blowups, tantrums, and frustrated words in kind, we can take a deep breath (or two or three) and say, "I know these math problems are challenging, but I know we can complete your homework step-by-step. Let's try this equation again." "I know you really want to buy that video game, but it is very expensive. If you would like to do more chores or baby-sit to earn the money, I will give you $25 toward your future purchase." Instead of giving into whining, "Oh, alright, you can have it! Just stop badgering me!" stand firm: "You haven't eaten dinner yet so I will not give you 25 cents for a gumball. You know the rules. If you're hungry now, let's find a healthy snack to tide you over."

- Use your actions to teach about patience. Let your children know when you are saving up for an item you want or holding off until Christmas. Help them to keep track of their bank accounts for college and other future plans. Give them a certain amount of spending money on a vacation, and let them know they must make purchasing choices wisely because once the money is gone, it is gone. Assist siblings in better understanding each others' viewpoints so they have more patience and tolerance of each other. Model this behavior in your marriage through empathy, listening, and respect. Say you're sorry when you lose your patience, and be patient with yourself. You may be the parent, but that doesn't mean that you don't have things to learn.

6. *Self-reliance*. I like to think of self-reliance as not only being dependent on oneself, but the ability to enjoy one's own company and to make decisions based on what is respectful to the self. Today, more than ever, self-reliance is an important virtue to practice. It allows time to be alone with one's thoughts and dreams. It allows contemplation and full engagement with an activity—reading, writing, listening to music, styling one's hair—because the individual is comfortable being alone. Far too often, our children feel the need to be entertained by us or the television. Constant stimulation is fast becoming the norm. But this lifestyle robs our children of developing their own creativity and imagination and, instead, encourages them to shy away from activities that are self-generated and to plug in to someone else's designed source of fun.

- Encourage self-reliance with your words. "Why don't you go outside and explore instead of parking yourself in front of the TV?" Give several suggestions, then let them make up their own minds. Use the word *no* as often as needed when your children lazily whine, "Why can't I watch more TV? There's nothing else to do . . . " Perhaps most importantly, nurture a positive inner voice that directs your children's feelings and behavior. If they think to themselves, "I can't draw" or "I'm too stupid to learn anything!" their confidence can plummet. And, as a result, so will their readiness to be self-motivated and to spend time devising projects on their own. If, on the other hand, children's inner voices are positive and affirming, they will feel more comfortable being self-reliant.

- Encourage self-reliance with your own actions. Do you pick up a book or magazine to relax? Take a hot, mineral salts bath? Or drop down in front of the TV? Do you have hobbies you engage in regularly? Quiet time? Or are you always going to the movies, to the pool, or to the store as a way to avoid time alone? Do you enjoy creative projects? Do you have the materials at home? As parents, our actions speak very loudly to our children. They emulate us. And how we choose to divide up our time and whether we put our time to its best use does not go unnoticed by our little ones. Perhaps you can encourage each other to take time out to simply be with yourselves, together? Parallel play is not just for kids!

7. *Self-motivation*. Self-motivation is a virtue that has many components. It is a sense of purpose, including a spiritual sense of "I know why I am here and what I have to contribute." It is a sense of direction that usually comes from inside, although it can be influenced or modified by external sources. However, it is not the same as being externally influenced: determining your actions by what

is believed to be expected of you by others. And it is the ability to take joy and pride in what you are doing instead of depending on outside validation.

- Encourage self-motivation with your words. Discuss rules with your family and use them as guidance tools to limit time spent on video games, television, and computer games. Stick to them. This way your children will know how to arrange their time and it will encourage them to find other things to do. "Your TV time is up. What do you think you'll do next?" "Shall we go to the library today?" "After you complete your homework, you can spend 30 minutes playing on the computer."

- Encourage self-motivation with your actions. Take quiet time to read together. Applaud your child's concoctions, Play-Doh creations, colorings (hang them up!), crafts, building creations, and dissections (radios, old cameras, etc.). Also, saying prayers together at night gives children the opportunity to speak about their own thoughts and wishes and to speak from who they are, not from pop cultural influences. Prayers can help us, as parents, to learn how to better assist our children toward the goals and desires they have for themselves as expressed, uncensored, through prayer.

8. *Honesty*. Honesty builds trust. We know we can rely on those who are honest with us. Deception, on the other hand, creates anxiety and hinders intimate attachments. After all, who can feel secure when he or she might be lied to or betrayed? Honesty takes courage in today's climate because unethical behavior is all around us. People

cheating to get ahead, lying to get what they want, and conning others to win. Unfortunately, these behaviors are no longer the exceptions to the rule.

- Be honest with your words. Don't lie to your children. Certainly there are instances when children need not hear the entire story. But it is important to let them know the truth in terms they can understand. Be honest when expressing your feelings. This lets children know they can expect honesty in their relationship with you, and that they, too, can verbalize their thoughts and feelings in an authentic way.

- Be honest in your actions. Return a wallet if you find one; let the clerk know she undercharged you for a grocery item; obey the speed limits and other rules designed to keep you and your family safe; don't hide a mistake even if you think it will anger someone; be honest with yourself by taking responsibility for your actions and admitting when you caused harm with any dishonest behavior.

9. *Cooperation.* Being part of a family requires cooperation if we are to be successful in achieving harmony and a sense of cohesive belonging. Cooperation helps us to work together as a team so that all benefit and we each get to experience what it means to be a part of a larger whole. Doing things for others by cooperating gives us pride in ourselves. The reward is in the doing, and we do not need to be repaid. Daily chores and tasks can be more fun when done together. In fact, cooperating with others, even members of our own family, can give us the opportunity to get to know them better.

- Use cooperative language for combining forces to reach goals. Use your smart words to engage others in collaborating with you to gain cooperation. Two heads can be better than one! When your children include others in their play, they are cooperating. Give them praise. Tell them they have good ideas.

- Cooperate with others so your children can learn by observing your actions. Are you flexible? Do you know how to include others in your plans? Do you engage your children in cleanup activities and group sports and games where cooperation is an essential element? Do you challenge your children by asking for group support to set up a tent, start a campfire, or prepare a boat for a fishing trip? Do you help to modify the playing rules for board games so children of all ages can join in? Remember: cooperation can be fun for everyone, and it helps to cultivate a sense of obligation to the higher good.

There are many more virtues that help to build a strong character and a positive self-concept as well as an optimistic outlook on life. Take some time to think about other virtues that are important to you: tolerance, fairness, trustworthiness, loyalty, and self-discipline, to name a few. Find simple and meaningful ways to incorporate them into your children's routine. You will be doing them a tremendous favor by preparing them for the future, not in terms of a recipe for success but rather by helping them to believe in who they are, knowing they have the skills to deal with whatever challenges life has to offer.

Resources

The Optimistic Child, by Martin E. P. Seligman, Ph.D.
New York: HarperCollins, 1995.

The Re-Enchantment of Everyday Life, by Thomas Moore.
New York: HarperCollins, 1997.

The Shelter of Each Other: Rebuilding Our Families, by
Mary Pipher. New York: Ballantine Books, 1997.

The Beacon Book of Quotations by Women, compiled by
Rosalie Maggio. Boston: Beacon Press, 1992.

*20 Teachable Virtues: Practical Ways to Pass on Lessons of
Virtue and Character to Your Children*, by Barbara C.
Unell and Jerry L. Wyckoff, Ph.D. New York: A
Perigee Book, The Berkeley Publishing Group, 1995.

*Teaching Your Children Life Skills (. . . While Having A
Life of Your Own)*, by Deborah Carroll. New York:
The Berkeley Publishing Group, 1997.

*The Family Virtues Guide: Simple Ways to Bring Out the
Best in Our Children and Ourselves*, by Linda Kavelin
Popov, with Dan Popov, Ph.D., and John Kavelin.
New York: Penguin Books, 1997.

The Seven Secrets of Successful Parents, by Randy Rolfe.
Chicago: NTC/Contemporary Books, 1997.

Raising Spiritual Children in a Material World, by Phil
Catalfo. New York: The Berkeley Publishing Group,
1997.

Raising a Family, by Jeanne Elium and Don Elium.
Berkeley, Calif.: Celestial Art Publishing, 1997.

*The Plain Truth of Things: The Role of Values in a Complex
World*, Colin Greer and Herbert Kohl, editors. New
York: HarperCollins, 1997.

10

Communication and Balance

Communication is an essential part of balance. Whenever two or more people cannot communicate effectively, things begin to go awry. Of course, I doubt I have to tell you this. Certainly, as a parent, you are all too aware of the mishaps, hurt feelings, and tension that has occurred on account of poor communication. (Not to mention the amount of communication it takes to get things back on track!)

The quality of our relating is usually defined by how well or how poorly we listen and respond to others. As a college professor once told me, "Communication involves two parts: speaking and listening." Although these two aspects of communication are very important, I would add another dimension that is often overlooked during the hustle and bustle of coordinating drop-offs and pickups, work schedules and school schedules: understanding. When we truly understand not only what is being said, but what our children think and feel, communication becomes an incredible form of intimacy, understanding, and connection—regardless of the topic.

The Power of Words

Harsh Words

The old saying "Sticks and stones can break my bones, but words will never hurt me" couldn't be more wrong. Harsh words can inflict irreparable damage. Words can unite and nurture closeness, and they can just as easily wound and divide. In her book, *The Argument Culture: Moving from Debate to Dialogue*, Deborah Tannen writes about the power of words and the ways in which our society has, in more recent times, shifted to arguing about issues instead of using the tools of communication to further knowledge and consensus. And, as Tannen can attest, the results are destructive and divisive, often creating an off-balance perspective. She writes: "Our spirits are corroded by living in an atmosphere of unrelenting contention—an argument culture . . . The argument culture urges us to approach the world—and the people in it—in an adversarial frame of mind." She goes on to say, "Conflict can't be avoided in our public lives any more than we can avoid conflict with people we love . . . But just as spouses have to learn ways of settling their differences without inflicting real damage on each other, so do we, as a society, have to find constructive ways of resolving disputes and differences."

The fact is, we live in a society that is becoming excessively focused on small-minded behavior and communication wherein words are used as weapons and irritants to "stir things up" instead of to educate or illuminate. It is essential, then, as parents, that we work to teach our children constructive ways to use words and the power they hold. By the same token, we must be careful to select our own words carefully—and I don't mean using civility as a superficial veneer of politeness that cloaks authentic communication. As parents, we hold a great deal of power, and our harsh, cavalier, insensitive words can inflict damage on those we cherish and love instead of fostering closeness and connection, which, if you are reading this book, is your true intention.

Real Words

Words without true meaning, honesty, sincerity, and integrity behind them are only words. For children, deception and false manipulation of words can be confusing, maddening, frustrating, and, more importantly, a betrayal of their trust and faith in us. (Just think of how off balance you feel when deceived or lied to by someone you're close to.) For this reason, authentic communication is essential. Now, this does not mean spilling out every thought we have or voicing every opinion we hold whenever we feel like it. It means being mindful of what we say to our children and how we say it; it means being truthful about our feelings, even the uncomfortable ones, without unloading them on our young ones. Most importantly, it means letting our children know we love them and that we can see their true selves—as conveyed by our words, actions, and expression—even when they are feeling sad, angry, lost, and not particularly pleasant to be around. In their book *Everyday Blessings*, Jon and Myla Kabat-Zinn write, "Being empathetic in the face of rejection requires us to not let our own hurt feelings get in the way of the pain our child may be feeling. In some sense, our children have to feel us holding on to them, no matter what repugnant (to our mind) spells come over them, no matter what dark disguises they try on." That is what is meant by being true to our word. Not only in terms of being reliable, but in terms of communicating to our children verbally (and nonverbally) that we will love them, no matter what.

The Importance of Listening

As a parent, you've probably noticed that listening to children is anything but a passive activity. It takes a lot of energy, focus, and attention to answer their unending questions; to explain scenes from a movie; to discuss their passions; to respond to their opinions in an intelligent way. My son, Alexander, was an early talker. At three-and-a-half months old he had a three-word vocabulary: "hi," "yes," and "baby." At 18 months he was asking me questions about death and dying, probing questions where an overly simplistic answer would not suffice. I remember my good friend Ginger riding in the car with us, completely impressed with my ability to concentrate on navigating the vehicle while I listened intently and produced intelligent responses to Alexander's drawn-out inquiries. "I don't think I'd have the patience," she confided. Just then, Alexander began directing his questions to his "Auntie" Ginger, and before she knew it, she was pondering subjects such as dinosaurs, rocket ships, nuclear power, ancient weaponry, exotic birds, and a lot of "How come?" While watching their exchange I noticed a growing closeness. From his questions and follow-up questions, she learned so much more about his inner world and private thoughts. She felt privileged that he would share all these things with her. Later, she remarked, "I thought my head was going to explode from thinking so hard, but it was *great!*"

Active listening changes both parties involved because it is an intimate sharing that has the power to transform, illuminate, and heal. As the writer Alice Duer Miller once said, "Listening is not merely not talking, though even that is beyond most of our powers; it means taking a vigorous, human interest in what is being told us. You can listen like a blank wall or a splendid auditorium where every sound comes back fuller and richer."

When we listen, actively, our children feel heard and respected. It creates the space whereby our silence gives them permission to speak from the heart, to try out their original ideas and self-discoveries, or simply to hear what cannot be expressed in words. It is important to remember that this type of listening takes time and mindful attention. We cannot do it when we are preoccupied with business and rushing around the house. We must slow ourselves down and make ourselves available to hear our children, especially when they are sending distress signals that cannot be ignored.

Active listening allows us to hear what our children do not say. As parents, we usually develop an intuitive ear for our little ones. We know when they're happy and we know when they're feeling out of sorts; we can sense when they're uncomfortable in a situation and when they are enjoying it; we can "listen" to their body language to find out who they like and who they don't. Why? Because when we listen actively, we are in tune. Our children are in our orbit and we are in theirs. We think twice—once for ourselves and once for our children.

Listening also means paying attention to your inner voice and teaching your children to listen to their own internal systems. Otherwise, the wise inner voice, the one that tells us to "slow down," say "no," say "yes," "connect," "create," "listen," "be tender," "make amends," "stand up," "rejoice," and so on, can become muffled and extinguished. As a result, you and your children spin further and further from your spiritual centers, making you out of sync and off balance.

True Understanding

In her bestselling book, *Kitchen Table Wisdom*, Dr. Rachel Naomi Remen talks about the necessity of what she calls "kitchen table wisdom." She describes kitchen table wisdom as stories that help us to reveal our true selves through the lens of our experience. She reminds us, "all stories are real." It doesn't matter if the same story would be told differently by someone else who was present at the time it occurred. It is still our story. And through our story, others have a chance to share our victories, losses, trials, and true loves. Whenever my parents' families get together (whether the Canadians in Canada or the Irish Midwesterners in the southern United States), I have the honor of being witness to the most amazing tellings of their childhood antics: teachers who were kind and those who brutalized their students in the days of corporal punishment; how my grandfather survived TB and while in the hospital wrote incredible love letters to the woman who would eventually become his bride; why I never met my genius Uncle Charlie, who was expelled in college for drinking wine and decided to travel the world wooing exotic women; how my Aunt JoAnn used to sing like a songbird—they even made a record of her in the 1940s—until she was diagnosed with diabetes; and how my Uncle Jerry spent so much time driving around the country in his low-riding Cadillac, always with a sink or bathtub roped down in the trunk. Such colorful and real characters whose lives do not follow a neat or predictable pattern or theme! No one, except maybe God, could have written their plays. As Dr. Remen says,

> When we haven't the time to listen to each other's stories, we seek out experts to tell us how to live. The less time we spend together at the kitchen table, the more how-to books appear in the stores . . . But reading such books is a very different thing than listening to someone's lived experience. Because we have stopped listening to each other we may have even forgotten how to listen, stopped learning how to recognize meaning and fill ourselves from the ordinary events of our lives. We have become solitary; readers and watchers rather than sharers and participants.

When we do not take time to listen to each other's real life stories, we miss out on truly understanding those we love. We miss out on understanding our family roots and the commonalities inherent in being human—what psychologists often call *existential understanding*, or, more simply put, "Knowing where you fit in the scheme of things." Yet, when we do take the time, our children benefit tremendously because they have the opportunity to use these stories for "seasoning their own stews" for better understanding of themselves.

The Importance of Feelings

We live in a society that places a disproportionate value on thinking over feeling. Not only do we view feelings as inferior to thinking, but we tend to attribute them more to women and girls, calling boys "sissies" and the like if they display them. Emotional qualities have come under attack in recent years and are being discouraged, not only in boys and men, but in women as well. It's as though our culture is suffering from a feeling phobia, and in a country largely run by thinking types, it is important to teach our children that feelings have worth, that they are valuable and essential to leading a balanced life with balanced relationships. Without an emotional vocabulary and knowledge of the emotional realms, it is difficult, if not impossible, to create lasting bonds with others. And, unfortunately, according to Daniel Goleman and other psychologists, the emotional realms can be stymied, and in some cases obliterated, with suppression or neglect. In his groundbreaking book, *Emotional Intelligence*, Daniel Goleman writes about the necessity of listening to our children's feelings:

> Prolonged absence of attunement between parent and child takes a tremendous toll on the child. When a parent consistently fails to show any empathy with a particular range of emotion in the child—joys, tears, needing to cuddle—the child begins to avoid expressing, and perhaps even feeling, those same emotions. In this way, entire ranges of emotion can be obliterated from the [child's] repertoire for intimate relations, especially if through childhood, those feelings continue to be covertly or overtly discouraged.

Why are feelings so important? Because they communicate the depth of our children's hearts and souls. They give voice to their inner life. They tell us how the world and the people around them affect them. Feelings tell us how our children are experiencing the events, friendships, and family life that surround them. And feelings often tell us when our little ones are asking for our help and guidance. It is our feelings that make us human. It is our feelings that give our soul expression. For children, knowing their feelings are respected validates who they are.

Feeling types need parental support when expressing the vast number of emotions that circulate through their bodies and inform their minds. Thinking types also need to learn the value of feelings for their own expression as well as respecting the emotional needs of others. As you might well imagine, it is often more difficult for thinking types to articulate and express feelings instead of closing them off or rationalizing them away. Yet the importance of being comfortable in the feeling realms and expressing feelings cannot be overemphasized. Feelings signal our children when they are hurt, stressed, frustrated, or confused; and feelings also allow our children to experience bliss, ecstasy, rapture, and joy. Keep this in mind: when one feeling is diminished or thwarted, it diminishes our children's ability to experience the others. So, if we discourage a healthy expression of anger, we will also be inadvertantly suppressing the ability to experience happiness, and so forth. To be whole, to be balanced, means having access to all feelings, the uncomfortable ones as well as those of a more pleasant variety. It is up to us, as parents, to nurture our children's emotional lives so they can shed tears of sorrow and tears filled with the sweetest of joys.

Taking Time for Feelings

It is very difficult, if not impossible, to take time for feelings while being habitually rushed and preoccupied. It simply doesn't work. Now, don't misunderstand me. I do not say this to induce guilt and remorse, nor do I say this to make parents feel small. I say this as a reminder to all of us. To support our children's emotional lives, we must be freed up enough to respond. We must be comfortable with difficult as well as cheerful emotions—allowing our children to not only speak about their emotions, but to express them as part of who they are. This takes time and attention. It takes the ability to listen, to empathize, and to understand. No small task, but greatly rewarding.

I remember when I was a new mother. My newborn infant could only express himself through a limited scope of emotions. Every time he squirmed in discomfort or cried, I responded. When I received criticism about my responsiveness to his feelings, I was taken aback. "You'll spoil him," they cautioned. "Let him cry it out," they warned. It hurt me to hear these things. Couldn't they see he needed my attention? Certainly, being this attentive was exhausting and time-consuming, but from what I could gather, this was all part of motherhood. I decided to stick to what I felt was best regardless of opposition from friends and well-meaning family members. Only later did I find statistical evidence to support what I had known all along, and you had better believe that I quoted my sources whenever I had to! Then I came across the words of the Kabat-Zinns, in *Everyday Blessings*: "Is adapting to *not* getting their needs met the way we want our children to develop 'independence'? Is shutting down emotionally and losing some of their aliveness and openness what we want for our children? Or do we want to teach them that their feelings count, that we will respond to them, that there are people who they can trust and rely on to be sensitive to them, and that it is safe to be open, expressive, to ask for what they need?"

Think about your own family. Are you comfortable with the expression of feelings? Or were you raised in such a way as to discount them or distrust them? Consider the following questions:

- Do you encourage feelings and help your children to name them?
- Do you prefer to speak intellectually to boys and more emotionally to girls, giving the impression that feelings are primarily the domain of women and girls? Or vice versa?
- Are you comfortable talking about feelings and finding healthy ways to express them? Or do they hold a low value in your family?
- Do you allow your children to contribute to a conversation and be included in decision making when appropriate, taking their feelings into account?
- Do you encourage your children to express unbridled enthusiasm for their ideas and the things that genuinely interest them? Or were you taught that exuberant emotional displays were unacceptable forms of bragging and drawing unnecessary attention to yourself?
- Are you comfortable with tears? Are you comfortable soothing tears and pains and hurts?
- Do you allow your children to express their points of view even if they differ from yours? Do you make an effort to understand how and why they feel about their experiences?
- Do you encourage prayer time? Do you create a sacred space where your children can say whatever is on their minds and in their hearts without receiving judgment, giving them the opportunity to speak from the power of their uncensored voices?

I remember when I was a sophomore in high school. I had just transferred from the Midwest and suddenly found myself surrounded by people I didn't know who, it seemed to me at the time, were not like me at all. I felt alone and alien to this new environment. To top it all off, I was required to take a driver's education class, which I imagined would be the closest thing to hell on Earth.

On our first of class we were introduced to the instructor: a tough-looking, loud-mouthed man with a crew cut whose nerves sprawled at the top of his skin. How he had managed to spend years contending with hormonally charged, unskilled kids behind the wheels of large automobiles was beyond me. Under these circumstances, it wasn't surprising that everything he said, every utterance from his lips, every detailed instruction, came out as a threatening yell. I winced every time he opened his mouth. Then, without warning, he asked all of us a question, and he wanted an answer, *now*!

"If you're driving along a mountain road and the only way to avoid a serious accident is to either drive into the side of the mountain or hit a cat on the other side, what are you going to do?" Immediately, everyone but me shouted out, "Hit the cat!" Hoping he wouldn't notice that I hadn't answered the question, I sat quietly rolling the scenario over and over in my mind. What to do? But, before I could come up with an answer I could live with, the ol' buzzard turned an eye on me and with an impatient growl demanded, "Well, what are you gonna do?!" Quietly, I responded, "I don't know." The other students laughed at me. But, to my surprise, this gruff old man announced to the rest of the class, "Don't laugh! To some people, running over a cat is worse than running into the side of a mountain. She'll have to decide for herself what she's prepared to do when the occasion arises." Because he respected my feelings so unequivocally, he was endeared to me. I knew he had taken a risk. He could have lost his standing of authority in front of all these immature and half-crazed adolescents. Instead, he gave them cause to think and consider someone else's feelings.

As parents, we have many opportunities to communicate our support for our children's feelings. In return, our children will be more inclined to share their feelings, and this connection will create more balance and wholeness in a world that often is fearful of the rich emotional realms.

Resources

The Argument Culture: Moving from Debate to Dialogue, by Deborah Tannen. New York: Random House, 1998.

Everyday Blessings, by Myla Kabat-Zinn and Jon Kabat-Zinn. New York: Hyperion, 1998.

Barnes and Noble Book of Quotations, edited by Robert I. Fitzhenry. New York: Harper & Row, 1987.

Kitchen Table Wisdom: Stories That Heal, by Dr. Rachel Naomi Remen. New York: Riverhead Books, 1996.

Emotional Intelligence, by Daniel Goleman. New York: Bantam Books, 1997.

How to Talk So Kids Will Listen, by Adele Faber and Elaine Mazlish. New York: Avon Books, 1980.

The Seven Secrets of Successful Parents, by Randy Rolfe. Chicago: NTC/Contemporary Books, 1997.

You Just Don't Understand: Women and Men in Conversation, by Deborah Tannen. New York: Ballantine, 1990.

11

Humor as a Way to
Create Balance

I was fortunate to have grown up in a family that had a good sense of humor. Not only did it lighten the tragedies and make them more interesting, but humor expanded our imaginings about the world by altering our perceptions. Both of my parents used to tell stories about the antics of their childhood that rivaled those of Tom Sawyer and Huckleberry Finn. I always felt close to them during these moments as I experienced a magical peephole into their pasts that revealed aspects of their personalities that were not always apparent. Sometimes they would use humor as a way to poke fun at their own foibles and vulnerabilities, allowing us to see their very human side with side-splitting laughter. Even now, in my own family, my two boys have formed a physical humor club called "The Cornish Game Hens." (Thank goodness we weren't eating eggplant the night they decided to name their comedy team!) In the tradition of the Marx Brothers, Charlie Chaplin, and the ever-popular Jim Carrey, the boys perform for us, bringing much guffawing and silliness into the household. It is this levity, through humor, that brings balance to all the members of the family. Why? Because laughter reduces stress, increases closeness, and affectionately communicates all kinds of insights and snippets of wisdom. Loretta LaRouche, author of *Relax—You May Only Have a Few Minutes Left*, was quoted in *Good Housekeeping* of September 1998 as saying, "Our minds are so cluttered with things we have to do, we don't witness our own comedy."

Seeing the Silly Side of Life

Fortunately, children are usually quite adept at finding something amusing in the daily aggravations of life. However, today's children are feeling more pressured. For most children, school and extracurricular activities do not allow them much time to relax and daydream. Life for many has become too serious and goal oriented. Getting silly is frowned upon as today's children are expected to be miniature adults. But it is important to remember two things: although some parents overschedule their children because they are anxious about "keeping up," others overschedule their children out of necessity. Usually the parents who fall into the latter category are also stressed. And, as a result, they make certain their children are continually on the go to alleviate some of the guilt associated with being away from the home. Under these circumstances, life can become incredibly stressful, and once again, humor can be the balm. Researchers tell us that mothers who laugh more than average usually have children who laugh more than average. And heartfelt laughter can be a bonding experience as well as an expression of kinship. It can close the gap that occurs when we don't have as much time as we'd like to spend with our children daily.

Balancing Stress with Humor
Think of ways you and your family balance out stress with humor. Do you play simply for the enjoyment? Do you take

time to be spontaneous and silly? Do you try to make everyday events like grocery shopping and rides in the car into fun and humorous activities? My parents excelled in these areas, and to this day I giggle when I think of my father's running monologue in the grocery store or my mother singing, "Good morning to you . . . We're all in our places with sunshiny faces . . . Good morning to you!" when I could scarcely extract myself from bed after the alarm had already sounded. But it is exactly these humorous moments and creative twists to the day that endeared them to me, and I have passed these on to my children—as well as my friend's children.

Certainly, I could arm you with all kinds of facts about humor's impact on stress—everything from lowering blood pressure to boosting the immune system's response—but the truth is, the proof is in the pudding. Humor keeps us sane. It balances out the stress that accumulates in all of our lives. It brings us together and keeps us healthy. As the old saying goes, "Laughter is the best medicine!"

Humor and Discipline

Humor is also a powerful antidote to the bad feelings that can arise when we scold our children or abruptly discipline them. Let's face it, when most of us think of disciplining our young ones we do not harken back to the divine root of the word: *disciple*. Rather, we think of punishment; loud, demanding voices; and others pointing out those things we are somehow doing wrong. In its most positive sense, however, discipline is about *teaching*; teaching our children values, boundaries, respect, and ways of doing things that can tool them up for life. Humor can bring out the *disciple*—the student who is waiting for our guidance—in *discipline*. The next time you have to reprimand a toddler for banging his toy on a buddy's head, try using an exaggerated clown face to communicate the pain and tears. It may seem silly, but remember, preschoolers have not mastered logic, nor do they fully comprehend cause and effect. By showing them broad strokes of the consequences of their actions, they can begin to piece together the results of hitting. Of course, it is important not to get too silly or your little one will think you are playing a game. Just "stay in character" as actors say, and illustrate, with your body language, how someone feels when he or she is knocked on the head.

NTC/Contemporary's Senior Editor Judith McCarthy shared some stories with me that are worth re-telling here as they are wonderful examples of ways to use humor as a form of discipline. Some of her friends have instituted zany theatrics usually performed at the dinner table in order to encourage their son to eat his green beans. They do the "green bean dance"; a happy dance to show their enthusiasm whenever he ingests those necessary but unpopular vegetables. Evidently, their son enjoys watching them dance so much that he forgets about the taste. It's definitely more fun for everyone to use the humorous approach rather than fight and, as most of us know, lose the battle. (It's a "you can lead a horse to water" kind of thing.)

Another way to use humor as a teaching tool is to choose your battles carefully. Ones that are not worth getting overly serious about are worth getting funny over. For example, your child empties every bottle of ketchup, soy sauce, mustard, and any other condiment she can find because she is conducting science experiments while you are taking a shower. Instead of yelling at her, even if you are angry, why not laugh at her ingenuity and curious mind and first ask her what her mixture of "chemicals" is to be used for. After taking a few minutes to see the situation through her eyes (she was not trying to make you run to the supermarket; rather, she was determined to repeat an elaborate brew recipe she read about in a Halloween book), you can explain to her that all future concoctions must be limited to the amount of ingredients that fill an average tablespoon. This way, you share in the joy of her creation while also teaching her about waste.

One mother told me about a funny method she used once to illustrate her displeasure regarding her twin boys' excessive potty talk. They were sitting at the dinner table, and, as usual, the boys started comparing the various foods to bodily excretions, each trying to outdo the other in a game of Who-Can-Be-More-Disgusting. Out of the blue, the mother picked up a handful of potatoes and threw them at the boys. They were in shock. They had been outdone by their own mother, and now she was laughing hysterically at the craziness of the situation. Soon the boys began to laugh, and, without words, their mother had made her point. That night, as she was tucking them in, she felt an opening where there had been none before, and she expressed her honest feelings to the boys, letting them know how upsetting and tiring it was to constantly hear such vulgar talk. Things were not perfect from then on, but they had changed for the better.

I distinctly remember my mother telling my brother that she didn't mind if he screamed or ranted or cried or begged, but she always ended with, "but don't whine!" We all know how incredibly annoying it can be. Why, it can turn you on your own child as your hands near his throat, determined to stop the dreadful noise! Next time your little ones whine, try this: gently pick up your children—one at a time—and tussle with them so they begin to laugh. Then, once the whines have passed, give them an intent listening ear to find out what they wanted to say. This is a good way to communicate to your children, in a nonverbal way, that whining isn't the best way to be heard.

Next time your child is grouchy, ask him if he's grouchy. When he says, "YES!" tell him that you'll join him and make exaggerated frowns, pouts, and stomping feet. If, on the other hand, you have older children who come back at you with a snide remark, "No, I'm not grouchy, I'm faking it. I'm actually in a good mood," look excited and say, "I'm in a great mood, too!" Then start imitating their grouchy behavior and declare, "This is fun!" If they're not in too foul of a mood, they usually smile and welcome the attention.

Anger, Fear, and Laughter

Consider this: one of the main sources of children's stress is parents' anger and stress. If you can laugh at life's difficulties, this will provide a valuable lesson. If you can opt for levity instead of power struggles, your children will learn how to better cope with differences. If you can teach your children the difference between focus and always being serious, they will find the joy that makes pursuits go more smoothly. Don't be afraid to get into their world. I recently saw a movie starring Robin Williams titled *Patch Adams*. It is a moving story based on the life of a young man who commits himself to a mental institution voluntarily after he attempts suicide. By interacting with the patients, he soon learns that he has a gift—an uncanny ability to bring out the best in others through humor, compassion, and such simple things as listening. During one scene, his roommate will not step down from his bed to walk across the room so he can use the toilet. As a result, he is holding his crotch and doing the uncomfortable I've-Got-a-Full-Bladder dance, which is making his bed squeak, thus keeping Patch Adams (Robin Williams) awake. Instead of getting angry with his roommate (even though it is apparent that Adams is irritated), he devises an ingenious plan to help his roommate summon enough courage to go pee. Because his roommate is frightened of imaginary squirrels (well, squirrels the rest of us can't see, anyway) that he believes are waiting on the floor to get him, Patch Adams makes his fingers into a gun and begins blasting away at each squirrel who lunges for them, eventually turning over the bed to protect them from the onslaught of killer squirrels. In the end, the laughter and absurdity prove to be the best ammunition against Patch's roommate's vivid fears—the ones that up to that point have been controlling him and narrowing his world to the parameters of his metal-frame bed. The scene is inspiring, to say the least. And yes, Patch Adams, with his unconventional antics, taught his friend about facing one's monsters. In a sense, he was the teacher. Yet, by approaching an annoying situation with spontaneity and wild laughter, he also learned the power of humor and its ability to reach others and improve the quality of their lives. He learned about humor's ability to transform individuals, even in adverse circumstances.

Humor, filled with respect and honesty, filled with good fun, allows us to be teachers to our children in the most creative of ways.

Resources

Marx Brothers films
Charlie Chaplin films
The Pink Panther movie series, with Peter Sellers

"The Far Side" cartoons, by Gary Larson

"Calvin and Hobbes" cartoons, by Bill Watterson

Ace Ventura: Pet Detective and *Liar Liar*, with Jim Carrey
(for older children with parents' discretion)

Patch Adams, with Robin Williams

Kids joke books and riddle books

Relax—You May Only Have a Few Minutes Left, by
Loretta LaRouche. New York: Villard Books, 1998,
quoted in Judith Newman, "Laughing Matters," *Good
Housekeeping* (September 1998), p. 105.

APPENDIX 1

The Myers-Briggs Personality Types

Introvert ———————————— Extrovert
Sensing ———————————— Intuitive
Thinking ———————————— Feeling
Judging ———————————— Perceiving

Here are brief descriptions of each personality type. I have tried to include the most striking qualities as well as the ones that accurately highlight each individual's unique traits. As you read each one, take time to see which aspects of the personality ring true to you. One particular type may stand out more than the others. Certainly, though, it is common to discover shared qualities between the various types. Again, no one fits neatly into one category. However, by examining the Myers-Briggs Type Indicator as well as the additional personality systems I have provided in Appendix 2, you can construct a unique motif of each child. Each child's motif will illuminate differences that can be learned from, shared interests, personal qualities that can complement relationships, and any inherent points of potential conflict. Thankfully, one of the great joys of being human is that some mystery always remains.

Personality Descriptions

"I" stands for Introvert and "E" stands for Extrovert.

"S" is for a Sensing preference and "N" is for an Intuitive preference.

"T" stands for Thinking types and "F" is for Feeling types.

"J" is for Judging (prefers structure) and "P" is for Perceiving (prefers options and possibilities).

Introvert

Introverts are not necessarily shy individuals. They simply draw their energy from an inward place inside themselves. Extensive social interaction can drain an Introvert, whereas Extroverts are stimulated by the company of others. Introverts need time to integrate any external stimulus, thus they are more inclined to spend time reflecting, reading, or meditating. It is essential for Introverts to have alone time in order to process the events and interactions that have transpired throughout each day.

Extrovert

Extroverts thrive on social interaction. They love to meet new people and experience new things. Their energy is usually directed outward and, although they also need time to re-group, they do not have as urgent a need as an Introvert. In other words, their batteries are just as easily recharged by being with others as being alone, depending on the level of their extroversion.

Intuitive

Intuitives are visionaries. They tend to make leaps in thought that often do not follow a linear progression. For this reason, they don't understand when someone tells them,

"You can't do that." For a determined Intuitive, they only need to figure out how to do it. Intuitives do not accept things as they are. Rather, they tend to see the infinite possibilities and creative ways to bring about change.

Sensing

Sensing individuals tend to be pragmatic and realistic. They work within the confines of what is and what can be measured. Unlike the Intuitive, Sensing individuals often proceed in a methodical way. They may reach the same conclusion as an Intuitive, but they will enter through a very different door (and often not as quickly). Sensors are linear and detail-oriented whereas Intuitives prefer to look at the big picture.

Thinking

Those with a Thinking preference tend to use logic and analysis to make assessments and reach decisions. They are more apt than those with a Feeling preference to give credence to facts and figures. They believe in objective material and may not think feelings are a valid approach to decision making.

Feeling

Feeling preference individuals are more likely than their Thinking counterparts to evaluate people, situations, and ideas from the perspective of their own value system. They view feelings as important and tend to include them in their decision-making process.

Judging

Judging personalities prefer order and structure. They like to make plans and take comfort in knowing the rules. They tend to be more methodical, always determined to complete a project once it's started. Usually, judging types make decisions quickly and easily. Unlike thir perceiving counterparts, they will not always seek out new information in order to consider all options. Instead, they will land on a course of action quickly and construct a plan to be followed step-by-step. In fact, once started, a plan is usually stuck to unless a convincing argument can be made for change. Judgers tend to be productive and responsible individuals who can be counted on to follow through.

Perceiving

Perceivers are the quintessential "go with the flow" types. Unlike judgers, perceivers often feel confined by rules instead of comforted by them. They like flexibility and spontaneity, and when faced with a choice, they prefer to leave their options open in order to gather more information rather than making a decision right away. Perceivers tend to be curious and inquistive, always asking a lot of questions. While perceivers love to begin projects, they do not always find it necessary to finish them; something that would be unacceptable to a judging type. Perceivers are usually playful. In certain instances they can be impulsive, not always looking before they leap. Change is not as frightening a prospect for perceivers as it tends to be for judging types because perceivers know a variety of opportunities will be made available to them, and it is only a matter of time before they choose one.

Enfj Personality Type

Enfjs are very people-oriented individuals. They care deeply about the feelings of others and are adept at anticipating other's needs. Outwardly affectionate and enthusiastic, ENFJs are eager to please and have a deep desire for harmony. Their belief systems are firmly intact. However, ENFJs have a strong ability to be flexible while clearly stating their feelings and values. They take things personally. As a result, their perspective is usually very subjective. They have a difficult time dealing with any type of conflict. In fact, they would rather appease others with a kind word than state their real feelings, which tends to make them diplomatic and personable.

ENFJs are creative and inuitive, yet they prefer to have things settled and organized. They plan their time for work and social events. They enjoy providing a variety of activities for others, including recreational activities. But, being highly flexible, they can just as easily follow others' plans and contribute in a way that draws those around them in. As a result, ENFJs are usually very popular.

ENFJs have an unusual ability to empathize with others. Yet they need to take care not to take on the problems of those around them so they feel as if the stresses and strains belong to them. Otherwise, they will find themselves overextended emotionally.

ENFJs have a bent toward the spiritual side of life, wanting to understand their place in the scheme of things. Intuitive, not only about feelings, but the motives of others, ENFJs do well to follow their hunches.

Activities That Encourage an ENFJ's Natural Strengths: Reading, speaking into a microphone, and addressing an eager-to-listen audience of loved ones. Putting on plays and puppet shows. Having access to costumes, hats, and props for improvisation. Being introduced to new, exciting topics of interest. Creating spiritual rituals out in nature or at home.

What Energizes an ENFJ: Being the center of a group of people and experiencing harmony, warmth, and fun. Having creative projects acknowledged by others. Having loved ones take a genuine interest in projects and participate when possible.

What Drains an ENFJ: Being exposed to cruel words or witness to verbal or physical abuse. Being isolated from others. Having plans constantly interrupted or changed abruptly. Not being able to express their dramatic side with acceptance from those closest to them.

What Relaxes an ENFJ: Ample "just being" time. Spending time out in nature just talking and answering questions about the meaning of life. Bath time with a tub loaded with toys and bubbles.

INFJ Personality Type

INFJs are highly intuitive and empathetic individuals who possess rich inner lives and vivid imaginations. However, because of their introverted natures, they often keep the treasures of their creativity buried deep inside, except with a few close friends they have come to trust over time. Of all the types, INFJs are most likely to demonstrate psychic ability, seeming to know events or details about another's life without knowing how they know. Being private people, INFJs might not come forward with intuitive information unless asked directly. Yet, because INFJs are very sensitive and their feelings are easily hurt, they are cautious with revealing their inner world at the beginning. Over time, however, INFJs will demonstrate more of their complex natures, sometimes surprising those close to them. Because of their sensitivities, they need calm, stress-free environments. If they are subject to hostility or constant criticism, they tend to lose confidence, become unhappy or depressed, and eventually become physically ill.

INFJs love fantasy play, writing, dramatic play, reading, music, and art. They tend to be highly creative yet are by no means purely quiet dreamers. When their personal values are challenged, they often respond with surprising forcefulness and passion, staying true to what they believe.

INFJs have warmth and integrity and they are often good at dealing with others. Large groups or too many social interactions at once can drain an INFJ. They are slow to warm to social situations, but once they feel comfortable they like to participate with others, usually one-on-one. Like other NFS, INFJs are sensitive and can easily get their feelings hurt by thoughtless comments or verbal attacks, especially by those they love. Although quiet, organized, and often self-sufficient, INFJs need plenty of reassurance when confronted with rapid change.

Activities That Encourage an INFJ's Natural Strengths: Hunting for treasures out in nature or at a $1 per pound "junk treasure" store to make into sculptures, writing—creative and journal writing, dramatic play, art, music, reading, and substantive storytelling, including oral traditions about family, Native American folklore, cultural myths from around the world, inspiring tales of historical heroes and ancient discoveries.

What Energizes an INFJ: Alone time, quiet companionship or parallel play, soothing baths with candles and soft music, having structured time to play.

What Drains an INFJ: Being around too many people for too long, too much noise and external stimulation, too much change too quickly or being confronted by constant change. Getting their feelings hurt by taunting or verbal attacks.

What Relaxes an INFJ: Alone time to engage in chosen activities such as reading or writing, soothing bath time, snuggling when they feel like it, being read to, having their head and feet massaged.

ENFP *Personality Type*

ENFPs are creative, curious, busy, and enthusiastic individuals. They have a large variety of interests, which they pursue with zeal. However, they may not always enjoy tending to the many details that accompany a project because they'd rather start something new. Keen observers, they need to mention each and every new impression they have or interesting thing they notice. Although they have the ability to focus intently on another person, they still remain cognizant of what is going on around them. ENFPs are naturally curious, and they tend to push limits and question authority, eager to find new solutions and possibilities that exceed the status quo.

ENFPs usually have a wide circle of friends, and they value their friendships a great deal. They enjoy having lots of people around them in engaging situations. Because they tend to think out loud, they frequently speak spontaneously or spout ideas they haven't considered for even a second before expressing them. Their infectious enthusiasm often draws others into their activities. However, they can become moody and act irrationally when overwhelmed or faced with too many details that are hindering them from moving on to another project or activity. Fiercely independent, ENFPs strive to express their unique attributes in all that they do. They enjoy dramatic play and similar activities such as interpretive dance, improvisation, and reciting spontaneous rhythms and stories, often adding a humorous twist and an exuberant voice. ENFPs take criticism to heart. They are loyal and caring friends, often demonstrating their feelings through generous actions: gift giving and little surprises. And, although ENFPs are only 5 percent of the population, they usually exert a great deal of influence because their personalities often have quite an impact on others. The combination of expressiveness, emotional intensity, and a strong desire to have authentic experiences creates a certain type of charisma that attracts others. In addition, ENFPs tend to be very perceptive and can offer insightful information that strikes others as being on target

Activities That Encourage an ENFP's Natural Strengths: Play acting; movement and dance; humorous, slapstick shticks; visiting the library; joining group activities such as dance troupes with a dramatic flair; reading their own stories out loud; jumping on trampolines; going on picnics or camping trips with close friends and their families; joining favorite cause groups such as the protection of animals, neighborhood cleanups, or planting for the environment.

What Energizes an ENFP? Interacting with new people as well as close friends, trying new rides at the amusement park, being able to pursue topics of interest. Being able to speak freely and being appreciated for their insights and ideas.

What Drains an Enfp? ENFPs need to express their ideas out loud and are very frustrated by people who either don't take time to listen or stifle their enthusiasm with endless objections or criticism. They also feel drained by projects that never seem to end, as well as projects that prevent them from beginning something fresh and more appealing. If they feel pressured to make a premature long-term commitment to any one project, class, or activity instead of being allowed to try a variety of experiences, ENFPs feel drained.

What Relaxes an Enfp? Soothing touch, arm tickles, massage, moving through water, having an in-depth conversation with a person they are close to, receiving assistance for finishing a task or project when they feel agitated or overwhelmed by the details, and moving their bodies either through exercise, dance, or creative movement.

INFP *Personality Type*

INFPs are best characterized as individuals with strong personal values and deeply felt emotional lives. It is very important for others to take an INFP's feelings into consideration when making decisions that affect them. INFPs are extremely sensitive, and they place a high value on maintaining inner balance and harmony in their lives. They like to dream and to imagine the meaning in every encounter and nuance of life. They need constant love, reassurance, and protection from a busy, high-pressure, and sometimes coarse and unfeeling world. If INFPs feel unloved or unwanted, they can become negative and moody, losing their optimism for a time. They often overpersonalize criticism and take everything to heart. It is not unusual for the parents of an INFP to feel as though they are walking on eggshells, carefully watching what they say and how they act around this type of child.

INFPs love to lose themselves in books: fairy tales, fantasy, love stories, classics, and mysteries. However, because INFPs are dreamers, they can have difficulty focusing and following through with homework and detail-oriented projects. The library can be an exciting place for INFPs as they can choose from so many topics, absorbing new information and a plethora of stories. They tend to be drawn to theater and the arts, and they often develop friendships with those more-sensitive and gentle individuals who share their interests. Although INFPs may appear reserved on the outside and even shy, they possess an intense capacity to care about others or to dedicate themselves to a cause.

Activities That Encourage an INFP's Natural Strengths: Browsing in libraries and bookstores, cultural arts, pottery and painting classes, age-appropriate museum exhibits, being taken on guided imagery tours of magical places, writing or drawing their feelings, poetry, playing alone.

What Energizes an INFP? Contemplation; receiving encouragement to ignore the messages of the outside world that come into direct conflict with an INFP's inner value system; getting lost in projects, books, and the beauty of art; building and creating block structures, sand castles, and homemade forts.

What Drains an INFP? Rapid succession of changes, not being notified of changes, rushing from one activity to the next, going from a quiet environment where they may be engaged in a favorite activity to a noisy, overwhelming store or mall. Not being respected and supported when they experience a roller coaster of emotions (which, for the INFP is not uncommon).

What Relaxes an INFP? Knowing they will not be interrupted; achieving focus through reading, writing, and listening to music and drifting with the sound; becoming engrossed in daydreams; living in a peaceful environment.

ENTJ *Personality Type*

ENTJs are an interesting mixture of logic and intellect coupled with creative and inventive impulses. They like to be in charge and often take an "It's my way or the highway" approach toward others. Not only are ENTJs demanding of themselves, but they can be demanding of others, frequently bowling over more-sensitive individuals who may not possess the same level of self-assurance. Because ENTJs may be so forthright in their opinions, they often forget to take others' feelings into account and may even regard others' feelings as silly and trite. However, ENTJs can learn to understand others' feelings intellectually even if they don't empathetically place themselves in someone else's shoes. They hold firmly to their viewpoint and may often speak with authority from an early age, convinced they are right.

ENTJs are determined individuals who like to gain mastery of the many things they try. They are easily bored and like to be exposed to new things every day. But their interests do not reside in the realm of the intellect and logic alone. ENTJs also love to engage in physical activities, even if they exceed an ENTJs capabilities. They love to listen to stories, especially those with adventure, intrigue, and more complex plots. And, whenever possible, ENTJs act out the drama of superheroes, intergalactic wars, and challenging battles. One important thing about ENTJs is that, although they enjoy being around other people and can interact with adults as easily as their peers, they often do not like to be touched, and they may be extremely vocal about their discontent.

Activities That Encourage an ENTJ's Natural Strengths: Accessing props and costumes for dramatic play, going to the library to look up answers for ENTJ's probing questions, visiting science museums that explain "how things work," pursuing sports they enjoy, working on tasks around the house that challenge them, telling their ideas and future goals with enthusiasm and finding ways to attain them.

What Energizes an ENTJ? Being exposed to new ideas and new challenges, whether physical or intellectual; demonstrating skills and prowess to the outside world; creating projects out of old clocks and appliances; watching the performing arts and emulating what they see.

What Drains an ENTJ? Too much routine and too little stimulation; being told that they must be more feminine (female ENTJs) and less sure of themselves so they avoid challenges and risks that, in their younger years, stimulate and propel them forward; being prevented from pursuing areas of interest; being isolated from others; having ideas thwarted.

What Relaxes an ENTJ? Being read to calms an ENTJ considerably, knowing exactly what the schedule is and feeling respected when it comes to making choices for family activities, having the freedom to pursue goals, setting the pace whenever possible, and being kindly encouraged to slow down and to be open to their gentler side, which helps them to achieve greater balance in their lives. Note: as with all NT children, cuddling and demonstrative forms of affection may irritate rather than soothe them. Although it may be difficult for us, as parents, to refrain from touching and patting an ENTJ, it is important that we respect their personal boundaries.

INTJ Personality Type

INTJs are fiercely independent children who may appear to be somewhat distant on the surface. Yet they care very deeply about those closest to them and may secretly wish to be understood (not necessarily "figured out"), especially by their parents. However, this is not always an easy task as their internal world is highly intellectual, logical, and complex; and they may be inclined to share only brief snapshots of the many elaborate connections they make. INTJs are intensely private individuals who resist being controlled by others, including their parents. They do not adhere to authority or rules unless they make sense to the INTJ. For this reason, INTJs can be challenging children to manage.

At their best, INTJs are precocious, early talkers who exhibit a command of language skills, using their talents to discuss topics that may seem advanced for their age. INTJs love to visit museums—art, natural history, and science museums—in order to learn more about how things in the natural world work. They ask a lot of questions and expect intelligent and logical responses.

Activities That Encourage an INTJ's Natural Strengths: Reading; going to libraries; spending ample time alone, especially after being bombarded with social or other externally stimulating situations; building with blocks; painting; working with clay; making crafts and creating collages; drawing; playing with chemistry sets and testing homemade or store-bought experiments.

What Energizes an INTJ? Being alone, focusing on projects or books for extended periods of time without interruption, thinking about different ways of doing things; and participating in individual sports such as skiing, gymnastics, tennis, martial arts, river rafting, and rock climbing.

What Drains an INTJ? External stimulation; being deprived of alone time; being exposed to too much talking and noise, especially in close quarters (cars, crowded commuter trains, shopping malls, and grocery stores); having to fight for their independence.

What Relaxes an INTJ? Closing the door on the hustle and bustle of the outside world and expressing themselves physically, as they are prone to the stress of striving for perfection, placing high demands on themselves. When they know what to expect, they feel much more relaxed; and, unlike some children, INTJs feel comfortable studying topics in incredible depth, as though their one-pointed focus is a Zen meditation.

ENTP *Personality Type*

ENTPs are best known for their exuberant energy, their love of new things, and their unusual sophistication, whether that demonstrates itself through an adultlike vocabulary, a keen eye for details while telling a story, or their advanced social and intellectual skills. They enjoy being the center of attention and are eager to elicit reactions from adults either through humor, dramatic renditions of adventure and fantasy stories, or with engaging conversation. ENTPs enjoy dressing up, pretending they are action heroes, animals, or make-believe characters. Their unadulterated enthusiasm often entices others to join them in their improvisations or carefully constructed plays. In addition, ENTPs like to use building blocks, toys with elaborate attachments, Legos, and a variety of art materials: colored pencils and charcoal, clay, paint, and glue.

Unlike their introverted counterpart, ENTPs enjoy surprises and are usually flexible when changes occur. They enjoy being outdoors and are fascinated by nature, wanting to know how the world functions. In fact, they are notoriously curious about the ways in which systems function, particularly the workings of the human body. This can lead to a plethora of questions about sexuality and other topics adults may find difficult to answer adequately enough to satisfy the probing mind of the ENTP. The ENTP's love for almost any topic is similar to that of the ENTP, and their natural effervescence can serve as a source of inspiration for others, engaging them in subjects they might otherwise dismiss or skim over.

ENTPs are constantly looking for ways to make things better, and they are often reluctant to do things in the same way, always on the lookout for new approaches to life. In fact, ENTPs are known for their ingenuity as well as their ability to solve problems quickly in ways others might not have thought possible.

ENTPs do not tend to have much patience. On the contrary, patience for these children is a learned skill, as is gentle and nurturing behavior. Being a *thinking* child as opposed to a *feeling* child means that ENTPs must receive logical explanations of why their behavior can elicit certain emotional responses from other children. With encouragement, ENTPs develop genuine empathy and the ability to wait their turn to speak (or for others to stop speaking) when they have a million ideas that feel as though they must be expressed all at once.

Like most NTs, the ENTP needs to be independent. Insisting that you do things for them undermines their belief in your confidence in them and can result in unnecesary squabbles. In short, they need to feel competent in every area of their lives, so it is best if ENTPs are encouraged to learn how to do things for themselves as early as possible. In later years, however, ENTPs may appear cavalier when it comes to following through with responsibilities and the more-mundane aspects of daily life simply because they become bored with routine and are more intrigued by starting something new. They also may overextend, not realizing the number of daily requirements involved in their many activities: sports, social clubs, student government, drama, and active social lives. And, like their introverted counterpart, the INTJ, ENTPs love to debate, skillfully finding the weaknesses in others' arguments, including those of their parents!

Activities That Encourage an ENTP's Natural Strengths: Drama, physical humor, putting on skits or slapstick routines, team sports, joining social clubs, scientific experiments, creating their own inventions, building with wood and other materials, having many different playmates, new and unusual things: Cirque du Soleil, travel, computer games with educational focuses, performing in front of others in a band, using traditional and nontraditional instruments.

What Energizes an ENTP? Having an audience, outlets for creative expression, having access to unusual building material (e.g., recylced wire and tubing), and arts and crafts. Being out in nature discovering insects, snowflake patterns, and new plants. Swim parties, picnics, and group activities, whether athletic or not.

What Drains an ENTP? Being rushed to get someplace on time. (ENTPs have little to no sense of time and order, and they find it interrupts whatever they are engaged in—although, again, they are usually flexible after their initial reaction to change.) Being alone or bored. Not having enough outlets for their creative and energetic minds and bodies and not being listened to—although, in all fairness, they can wear their parents out with constant questioning and debate.

What Relaxes an ENTP? Engaging in games with friends, keeping the number of activities at a manageable level (with the help of family and teachers), being read to, storytelling (around the campfire is great!), music with songs that tell a story or have a curious twist at the end or a song that is made up as it goes.

INTP *Personality Type*

INTPs are only found in 1 percent of the population, so for many parents of this type, raising an INTP child can be a bit of a challenge. INTPs are highly introspective, and like most NTs, they are logical thinkers, fiercely independent, and often prefer the company of their own thoughts to being around others. Authors David Keirsey and Marilyn Bates describe the INTP in their book *Please Understand Me:* "One word that captures the unique style of an INTP is *architect*— the architect of ideas and systems as well as the architect of edifices." Although INTPs are logical and analytical, they do not often take ideas, facts, and opinions at face value like many STs. Rather, INTPs are creative and original thinkers, unimpressed by authority based on rank, title, or status.

INTPs need lots of room to explore and develop their unique approach to the world. Certainly, they march to the beat of a different drummer. Being introverted, they may appear to be very serious even as an infant or toddler. And, more than any other type, INTPs are often aloof, stoic, and impersonal. In fact, like most NTs, they are not typically demonstrative and outwardly affectionate and can become easily fatigued by social interaction.

INTPs love to learn new things and are interested in mastering a variety of skills, sports, and subjects. However, they may not readily share their thoughts or their experiences with others, choosing to save their verbal expressions for questions and colorful descriptions of events. To others they may appear shy and cautious, but if they let someone into their world, usually one-on-one, one will discover the many internal connections INTPs make. They are natural inventors and enjoy taking things apart—everything from elaborate jewelry to electronic equipment. And they may play with toys in an unconventional way. It is very common for INTPs to experience short spurts of energy followed by quiet and solitude. Their need for action and social interaction is met in bursts that are unpredictable in nature and come in erratic intervals. Like all NTs, INTPs do not respond to strong showings of emotion to persuade them. Rather, they respond to direct, flawless logic and may exhibit confused or condescending behavior when confronted with emotional outbursts from their parents.

Activities That Encourage an INTP's Natural Strengths: Exploratory play, solitude, long stretches of time to investigate topics and activities of their own choosing, often within their own rooms. Puzzles, building materials, creative toys, and computers stimulate INTPs' active minds. They love solving problems and making things work in new ways. Although quiet and seemingly reserved, INTPs are very physical and enjoy challenging themselves with sports such as rock climbing (i.e., climbing on counters), gynmastics, and exploring on foot.

What Energizes an INTP? Open-ended activities. Any topic, talent, or skill that inspires them to apply their creative analytical abilities. Exploring, climbing, tinkering with mechanical devices. In fact, as Paul D. Tieger and Barbara

Barron-Tieger, authors of the book *Nurture by Nature*, point out, "Parents of INTPs are advised to stay ever alert for some subject or endeavor that has captured their INTP's interest so they can support his or her continued pursuit of it."

What Drains an INTP? Being rushed, moving too quickly from one activity to the next in succession, too many social interactions, being forced to join in social situations before they are comfortable or feel confident about knowing what the activity is or what is going on, being held back from exploring and mastering a skill or talent of interest.

What Relaxes an INTP? Privacy, being given ample time to focus on projects of interest, bath time (supply bubbles for experiments and play), being out in nature to explore.

ESTJ Personality Type

ESTJs are keenly aware of external rules, structure, and environment. They are very responsible and often insist that procedures and details be handled carefully and correctly. Being literal and practical minded, they tend to jump to conclusions quickly, not always receptive to differing points of view.

As infants, ESTJs are often restless and fidgety, preferring physical movement such as rocking, swinging, or being in the stroller to sedentary activities. They are outgoing and busy children, often having a propensity toward self-directed goals. ESTJs love to interact with others and seem to enjoy being around a variety of people. In fact, more-cautious parents may feel uneasy with ESTJs' ease with introducing themselves to anyone new, including complete strangers! They are extremely detail minded and like to memorize stories, multiplication tables, and names and feel very proud of themselves whenever they have mastered an activity. ESTJs thrive on order and often assume leadership positions, certain that they know "the right way" to play a game, ride a bike, and so forth. Although comfortable with others, ESTJs tend to be matter-of-fact emotionally and are not easily affected by the actions or words of their peers. And, in spite of being talkative, ESTJs do not verbalize their feelings openly and freely. In fact, they may discount or minimize their emotions, opting to take an "It doesn't bother me" or "I'm tough enough to handle it" approach.

Many children do not develop a deep appreciation for family rituals and traditions until later in life, but ESTJs like to be involved in preparation for holidays and functions with relatives down to the smallest detail. As adults, they are likely to be the ones who show up for class reunions, annual picnics, and work-related social events.

ESTJs are very energetic, people-oriented children, and it is important for parents to give them plenty of physical outlets to release their energy. Otherwise, ESTJs become easily bored and frustrated and may be prone to tantrums, especially if they are tired or too wound up. Although active and outgoing, ESTJs are not always open to new adventures simply because they have a strong need to be in control. Authors Tieger and Barron-Tieger describe it best: "They often claim they don't like something before they have even tried it. Their first reaction to a new food, game, toy, vacation spot, or experience is almost always negative. If they have no firsthand, personal experience to rely on, they feel threatened, and their first response is to say no." It is important for parents to be respectful of the ESTJs' tendency to balk at new things. Forcing children to move into new situations before they are ready can be detrimental to their self-esteem and can foster a feeling that they can't trust their own timing or natural inclinations.

ESTJs excel at team sports. They listen well, follow directions, and have a strong sense of their bodies—and they enjoy winning. Respected by their peers for their physical prowess and ability to learn the rules of the game quickly, ESTJs often excel in the physical arena.

Activities That Encourage an ESTJ's Natural Strengths: Team sports, playing outdoors (especially at a favorite, well-known park), stamp collecting, rock collecting, baseball-card collecting (they are passionate collectors), cooking and following recipes, crafts, being in nature, drawing, painting, bike riding, and playing with others (ESTJs need social contact and a variety of ways to keep continuously busy).

What Energizes an ESTJ? Being around others, especially those they are familiar with, being involved with almost any family activity—cooking, learning to brush teeth, how to work the vacuum cleaner, preparing for holidays and get-togethers—sports and physical activity, mastering a skill or finishing a project (puzzles, building a castle, Legos, etc.).

What Drains an ESTJ? Not getting enough sleep, being forced to remain quiet and still for extended periods of time, not knowing what the plans are for the day or having too many open-ended plans, being pushed into new experiences too quickly (ESTJs may appear confident because of their physical and active nature, but they do not like to jump into unfamiliar situations), and dealing with too many abstract ideas at once because ESTJs are very logical and factually minded.

What Relaxes an ESTJ? Movement (rocking, swinging, climbing), riding a bike, structure and familiarity, knowing the rules and what is expected, feeling included and in control, receiving concrete tasks and assignments (with details they can master and facts they can memorize), knowing they are not responsible for everything, and knowing homework, deadlines, and projects are fully completed so they can go have fun.

ISTJ *Personality Type*

ISTJs are usually serious children who possess a quiet intensity, a logical mind, and a memory for detail. They tend to bond to only one person, usually their mother or father, and are not always receptive to the social advances of those they do not know.

ISTJs have a strong body awareness. Not only can they make distinctions about smells, tastes, and textures, but they also like to keep themselves running on a regular schedule, as they need adequate food and sleep to maintain their energy. ISTJs often need more time alone than others to rest and spend time with their own thoughts. In fact, ISTJs can seem cold and remote because they are often fully engaged with a dialogue that runs perpetually in their minds, and their power of concentration is intense. They can easily tune out external stimulus, including others' conversations and questions. When others try to break an ISTJ's concentration, they are frequently met with irritability and a gruff impatience. However, ISTJs tend to be very polite and respectful children overall. They simply need their alone time to be respected as much as possible.

IstJs are not apt to display a penchant for drama. On the contrary, they enjoy routine and sensible practicality. They have a strong sense of duty and responsibility and expect to be taken at their word. IstJs are traditional types who tend to be loyal to social institutions as well as family institutions. Often preoccupied with finances and maintaining the status quo, istJs do not invite broad fluctuations of change into their lives. In fact, change is often very difficult for them unless they receive ample warning time and explanations about why the change is necessary.

As introverts, istJs are slow to warm in social situations, and, more often than not, they prefer one or two close friends as well as the company of their family. At their best, they are organized, efficient, punctual, and reliable children with an ability to research topics with accuracy and arrange factual information in an orderly way.

Activities That Encourage an IstJ's Natural Strengths: Playing with a variety of textures; collecting coins, cars, and other items of interest; reading; having access to books of facts and records (encyclopedias and *Guiness Book of World Records*); computer programs with interesting facts about finance; studying the human body and the physical world; engaging in family activities without too many outsiders; swimming; resting on a porch and playing board games or playing outside games where the rules are established and clearly followed; being one-on-one with a close friend.

What Energizes an IstJ? Alone time, adequate food and sleep, knowing exactly what is scheduled each day, being given projects with explicit directions and clear objectives, having a sanctuary wherein they can dwell on their own thoughts (a private room, a hammock set between two trees, a playhouse).

What Drains an ISTJ? Abrupt changes in schedule and plans, being pushed into social situations and new experiences before they have had adequate time to comprehend what is taking place, not getting enough sleep or adequate nourishment, being given too many tasks—especially openended ones—at once, being expected to pretend they like something or someone when they don't, feeling isolated from family.

What Relaxes an ISTJ? Plenty of quiet time alone, watching a favorite TV show on a regular basis, massage to still the incessant chatter in their heads, sharing their activities with someone who takes genuine interest in them (one of the best ways to get close to an ISTJ is to do what they prefer doing so their interests don't have to compete with anyone else's).

ESFJ *Personality Types*

ESFJs are often thought of as the most sociable of all the types. Their lives gravitate around others and they thrive as part of a close-knit, loving family. ESFJs enjoy doing things for members of their families and they develop close friendships early on in life. Service-oriented individuals, ESFJs need to receive praise and considerable appreciation for their efforts; otherwise, they are likely to feel uneasy or even hurt. For this reason, it is important for parents of ESFJs to express their love and demonstrate how pleased they are by the ESFJ's efforts. ESFJs usually need reassurance, as they are highly sensitive to the emotional states and opinions of others and may tend to personalize negative responses, especially if these responses are made in reference to something or someone they cherish, or direct criticism of them.

ESFJs are conscientious people who prefer order, structure, and consistency in their routines. They like things to remain the same. However, when it comes to social interaction, ESFJs are rarely timid. In fact, they extend themselves to others freely and will initiate games with a new playmate without hesitation. So social are ESFJs that they are often thought of as *chatty*, because they will enthusiastically discuss their opinions, thoughts, and feelings. Should a conversation become more philosophical, abstract, or scientific, an ESFJ may lose interest or become more reserved.

ESFJs are sensitive children who unabashedly express their affection at regular intervals during the day. They want and need lots of physical attention: hugs, kisses, holding hands, snuggling, sitting on laps, and caresses. However, simply because ESFJs are sensitive does not mean they are necessarily calm and quiet. On the contrary, ESFJs can be boisterous individuals who beg for their parents' and siblings' attention—"Watch me!"—and blurt out their ideas and feelings with a flurry of interruptions to others' conversations.

ESFJs have a strong need for harmony and tend to go to great lengths to avoid conflict and confrontation. They are easily overwhelmed by stress and tension and will show physical and emotional signs of distress if equilibrium is not restored. Although generally possessing a sunny disposition, ESFJs can exhibit a pessimistic attitude that can be contagious, making others worry about possible future events.

ESFJs have lots of energy for physical activities such as bike riding, roller blading, sledding, jump rope, four-square, and the like. Yet, more than any other type, ESFJs seem highly conscious of gender-specific play: girls play with hair, makeup, and Barbie dolls, while boys focus on violent video games, action hero games, and rough and aggressive chase games. Although ESFJs love to play, they tend to complete homework and other tasks first, taking things in their "correct" order: work *before* play.

Activities That Encourage an ESFJ's Natural Strengths: Outdoor play; playing with makeup, hair accessories, and arranging outfits for the school week (for girls); sports; music; art; social clubs; performing for their parents and other family members; having access to a variety of playmates, perhaps in a play group, Brownies, 4-H clubs, and so forth. ESFJs also love to spend time with animals, grooming, caring for, and playing with them (and, of course, being complimented by others for how well they are doing and how loving they are).

What Energizes an ESFJ? Being around friends and family, meeting new people, talking (and talking and talking!), playing outdoors, having an extremely receptive audience to perform for, receiving lots of hugs and kisses and obvious signs of love and affection, receiving an abundance of reassurance during challenges and moments of fear and doubt, completing a task, being in a harmonious environment.

What Drains an ESFJ? Conflict, stress (especially prolonged stress, as they value order, structure, and consistency), being left out, holding on to grudges (which an ESFJ is prone to do), dealing with an overwhelming amount of abstractions (those presented in math class, philosophy, and science), feeling taken advantage of and not appreciated for their efforts, criticism.

What Relaxes an ESFJ? Movement (rocking, swimming, or floating in water, swinging), being held and rocked by those they love; cooking, cleaning, and caring for a house along with either of their parents; having a steady, regular routine; massage or head rubbing; playing with hair (brushing or styling); reading a book series in order.

ISFJ *Personality Type*

ISFJs are gentle, loving, and considerate people who need a sense of order and predictability in their lives. They frequently take things at face value, having a literal approach to life. ISFJs need to feel in control of themselves to feel free enough to open up and experience new things. They are typically self-contained and even tempered when things are going the way they expect. However, most ISFJs can become upset and frightened by rapid or unexpected changes. Like ESFJs, ISFJs also need a loving and nurturing family structure, as harmony and balance in personal relationships is deeply important to them. As children, they are affectionate and loving. And, like most SFs, they are demonstrative with their feelings, wanting to hold hands, sit in their parents' laps, and share family intimacies: secrets, private humor, and stories.

Sensitive children, ISFJs often cry easily and are prone to getting their feelings hurt at the slightest cause. They will go to great lengths to avoid repeating a difficult experience, especially if it involves another person. In fact, ISFJS will become reticent about interacting with an individual with whom they have had a negative experience previously. If they are frightened by something, whether it be an insect or getting soap in their eyes, ISFJS can become very reactive to the object, indeed almost phobic, needing ample reassurance from parents and caregivers that they will not be harmed. It is not advisable to push these children into any situation faster than they are comfortable (a good rule of thumb for all kids), because it will only create more resistance and withdrawl. And, like most children, ISFJS react negatively to criticism and harsh words. Rather, they need to be lovingly reassured and encouraged and reminded that they can succeed even when they feel reticent and fearful.

ISFJs appreciate the simple things and are known for their ability to take good care of their possessions. They may like to collect a variety of objects: sports cards, cars, rocks and crystals, and so forth. They are also great animal lovers, enjoying interacting with and caring for a pet. Feeding and caring for an animal gives them responsibility they enjoy. Like other SFs, ISFJs tend to prefer gender-specific activities and toys. They are not always comfortable with boys playing with dolls or girls liking trucks. Indeed, they are somewhat conventional children who do not dream about what could be or the life they could have but tend to follow in their parents' footsteps. What is known is comfortable to them, and this attitude continues into adulthood. ISFJs are not likely to become rebellious or challenge the system. However, they might try something to secure their place in a group, then return to more traditional approaches to life shortly thereafter. At their best, ISFJs are gentle, loving, and warm people who treat others, especially those they love, with great respect. They are neat and orderly and, if the central aspects of their lives are secure, will become more and more adventuresome and willing to take risks to expand the parameters of their life.

Activites That Encourage an ISFJ's Natural Strengths: Swimming, biking, team sports (if they feel respected and appreciated as a member of the group), building collections (coins, fossils, marbles, jewelry, beads, sports cards, etc.). Touch is very important to ISFJs (massage, backrubs, arm tickles), and they enjoy sensory stimulation in normal doses. They love to be read to, sung to, and rocked in order to decompress after busy days at school or at play. Puzzles, arts and crafts, drawing and painting—projects that end with a result they can be proud of.

What Energizes an ISFJ? Being with close friends and family, spending time alone, straightening the house, being outdoors, reading books or the paper, knowing what is expected and knowing exactly what will happen, intimate conversations, soothing touch, soaking in a hot tub.

What Drains an ISFJ? Too much stimulation, being away from a close circle of friends and relatives for extended periods, too much change too quickly, being pushed to excel, entering into a new situation without sufficient support or advanced warning, criticism, feeling unloved and unappreciated.

What Relaxes an ISFJ? Structure, having things in place, time alone to putz, reading, soaking in a tub or a jacuzzi, massage, intimate touch (hugs, kisses, backrubs), being with familiar faces in familiar places.

ESTP *Personality Type*

ESTPs are children of energy and action. They often throw themselves into new situations without any concern for the outcome. To many, ESTPs seem impulsive, especially because they are prone to push the limits. They have a strong need to explore the world and acquire a variety of new experiences. They are usually charming, witty, and clever individuals who require explicit direction from their parents. Otherwise, ESTPs will find a way to gain what they want from a person or a situation. Always several jumps ahead of another's actions and motivations, ESTPs can appear to have a great deal of empathy when, in fact, they are actually masters of reading body language and other signals, and they respond accordingly. ESTPs need plenty of physical exercise and freedom or they can become cagey and irritable. They love to meet new people and seem to become more energized by simply being the life of the party. They enjoy physical humor and making others laugh. Sometimes they are so full of energy, they bounce off the walls and are unstoppable when it comes to expressing themselves verbally.

ESTPs are very adventurous children. They are firmly rooted in the present and, for this reason, they may not often consider the consequences of their actions. Fortunately, they bounce back easily and are not thwarted by past mistakes or misjudgments. Usually the first to try new things, an ESTP will take dares and risk chances other children would never consider. They can live on the edge at times, narrowly escaping disasters or creating innovative new approaches. As one might expect, ESTPs love to be part of the action. Even as toddlers, they will beg to join in the fun of the older children's games.

ESTPs do not like to be restricted. They often prefer to run around naked simply because clothes feel too restrictive. They do not like to be told that they cannot do something—it infringes on their personal freedom. It is important to channel the exuberant energy of the ESTP, otherwise, they will turn their talents to not-so-constructive ends. If they are prevented from doing what they want, they can become volatile and prone to emotional outbursts. However, on the whole, ESTPs are vivacious and have a positive attitude. Comments and criticism do not seem to affect them. Rather, their emotional expressiveness seems to stem from feeling left out of the action, not being included, and being held back from adventures and journeys they wish to embark on. Verbal reprimands aren't always very effective with ESTPs. In fact, they can even get in your face and ask a million questions only to turn around and do the very things you just told them not to do. Actions speak louder than words, and it is important to remember to take quick action by stepping in to remove dangerous objects or lift the child out of the way of danger. But parents must remember not to become too rough with an ESTP, because ESTPs will quickly emulate any aggressive behavior and may begin to use it as a method for getting what they want with other children, including their siblings.

ESTPs love to laugh. Physical humor is a real joy for ESTPs because they get an opportunity to combine their need to move with their love of fun and laughter. They often become known as class clowns because they have difficulty sitting still for long periods of time and may use tactics such as pulling hair, poking students with pencil erasers, and whispering as a way to keep themselves active and entertained.

ESTPs do not tend to enjoy abstract thought. Rather, they will approach the world very literally, accepting what is on the surface without asking the deeper questions. It is not unusual for ESTPs to bring home a report card that does not adequately reflect their true intelligence. ESTPs do not always apply themselves in academic settings, not because they are being difficult, but because they are often bored with theories and the passive studying of subjects. Although not always motivated to be scholars, ESTPs will excel in areas they are excited by: troubleshooting, entrepreneurial endeavors, and search and rescue (divers, avalanche teams, and river guides).

Activities That Encourage an ESTP's Natural Strengths: Team sports (although they may not stick to one sport over a long period of time simply because they feel they are missing something if they don't try a variety of athletics); following fashion trends; shopping; starting a small, neighborhood business (selling lemonade, candy, and the like); watching Charlie Chaplin and Marx Brothers movies (like NTs) to study and imitate physical comedy; working with their hands with clay, Legos, paint, and so forth. ESTPs love to be engaged with other people in games such as "Capture the Flag," "Red Rover," and "Tackle the Man with the Ball."

What Energizes an ESTP? Movement; physical play; dancing; swinging; pushing the merry-go-round; adventures such as rock climbing; amusement parks (the more thrilling the ride the better); becoming a superhero (replete with costume and all mannerisms); being around other children; playing out in nature, where they can climb, explore, and run to their hearts' content; digging in mud or sand; playing at the beach.

What Drains an ESTP? Sitting for extended periods of time, listening to abstract theories and continual hypothesizing, being physically restricted or being stuck indoors, solitude, too much quiet that is void of activity, and reading at great length, especially if there is no action in the story.

What Relaxes an ESTP? Knowing exactly what the boundaries are, using up their physical energy, being rocked, using their hands and bodies in water play, digging, reaching into tide pools, planting in the garden, and excavating dirt for buried treasure.

ISTP *Personality Type*

ISTPs are the epitome of action-oriented individuals. They have an uncanny ability to learn through their bodies in the moment. They do not like to plan or prepare. Rather, they will pit their skills and physical prowess against almost any situation or individual. They thrive on excitement and are among the greatest risk takers despite frequent injuries. ISTPs enjoy racing (cars, bikes, running), surfing, sky diving, and other daredevil sports such as rock climbing, hang gliding, flying planes, bow hunting, and the like. Weaponry and the skill of executing the instrument with mastery are common interests of ISTPs. Like many children, especially boys, ISTPs show a fascination with being a weapon virtuoso and will exhibit these traits in their play. The combination of using their physical skills with the thrill of combat is appealing to many ISTPs. As Kiersey and Bates point out in *Please Understand Me*, "Indeed we must call ISTPs the tool artisans, for they above all others command the tool and bend it to their impulse. But again, ISTPs—personified in Michelangelo and Leonardo da Vinci—work (or better, play) with their tools on personal impulse and not on schedule." Whether the tool is a sword or a scalpel, the ISTP is strongly adept, a natural, at wielding it.

Because ISTPs are so physically oriented, they prefer to communicate through action instead of words. They are often quiet, and although they enjoy being with one or two close friends, ISTPs are soon drained by navigating the politics of any group dynamics. Their lack of verbal skills is sometimes mistaken for *dyslexia*, or a blanket use of the term, *learning disability*. Yet it is evident that their greatest strengths are in the physical realms—and in this arena, ISTPs illustrate remarkable precision.

ISTPs love their freedom and resist being reined in. They may not defy a teacher or parent openly. Rather, the defiance will be exhibited in their bodies and the steadfast way ISTPs hold their eyes. Not surprisingly, ISTPs have difficulty sitting still for extended periods of time. They often show a penchant for math and science (especially hands-on science), and usually like creative writing and abstract literature the least.

ISTPs are intensely private and are often out of touch with their feeling side. They rarely confide in others about their emotions or responses to events until they have spent some time alone and are ready to talk to someone they trust. They value directness and may have to learn tact and empathy in dealing with others. If reasons for others' show of feelings or more-sensitive responses to things are not logical enough for the ISTP, he may label them as "stupid" or "dumb."

IsTPs love being out in nature, having ample time to play in the dirt and mud, collect insects and rocks, and climb trees. Rope swings that they can use as jumping-off places into ponds and rivers are great fun for ISTPs. Nature is an unending playground for these children, and the treasures they find, they will, inevitably, want to bring inside and keep in their rooms. IsTPs are not known for neat and tidy bedrooms. They reserve their precision for other, more adventuresome hands-on activities.

Activities That Encourage an IsTP's Natural Strengths: Being outdoors, rock climbing, hiking, backpacking, skiing, surfing, boating, dirt-bike racing—just about any sport that excites them. IsTPs also enjoy hands-on activities such as puzzles, water play, experiments, mixing concoctions, Legos, drumming and creating rhythms and music.

What Energizes an IsTP? Being with other adventurous types, doing new and exciting things, working with tools, time alone, mastering a skill or use of a tool or instrument, learning more concrete math concepts, experimenting with science, and exploring out in nature (e.g., camping trips, canoe and raft trips, whale watching).

What Drains an IsTP? Being surrounded by too many people at once, not getting any alone time to ponder and play, sitting for extended periods of time, being expected to listen to long-winded discussions, feeling restricted and held back from exploration and adventure.

What Relaxes an IsTP? An occasional backrub (ISTPs are not generally cuddly children), being alone, bath time, feeling accepted for their nonverbal private and physical temperaments, focus of attention through the body (rock climbing, gymnastics, sword fighting—sports with action coupled with precision).

Esfp *Personality Type*

EsFPs are very witty, cheerful children who exhibit the traits of a well-bred conversationalist. They enjoy engaging others in their lively banter, and they never seem to be at a loss for friends. EsFPs enjoy the best life has to offer, whether it be food, clothes, furniture, automobiles, or so forth. Life to EsFPs is to be lived to the fullest. They do not worry about dark fates befalling them because they prefer to look on the bright side. EsFPs may deny the severity of certain events, however, avoiding the anxiety it causes them until it is pushed up into their faces. But, the first chance EsFPs get to diverge into a more enjoyable activity as a means of avoidance, they will take it.

Naturally generous, EsFPs will generally give without expecting anything in return—and this includes love. They ooze with amusing wit and good humor, having no need to keep a tally of favors. Occasionally, others may manipulate EsFPs or take advantage of their good-natured merriment. But, with time, EsFPs develop a greater level of common sense.

EsFPs can be dramatic and enjoy excitement in daily life, relationships, and, later, in their careers. The performing arts hold appeal for EsFPs. Yet they are just as likely to become nurses, social workers, and businesspeople. Scholarly education does not usually hold EsFPs' attention, as they prefer to have more breadth than depth.

EsFPs can be very affectionate and demonstrative of their love and warm feelings for others. They express themselves in an exuberant fashion, often vocalizing (or declaring) that someone is a friend or a special person in their life. ESFPs seem to always like everyone, and their manners and acts of kindness seem to be innate.

Other children may be homebodies or prefer to remain in environments that are familiar to them, but ESFPs love to travel and visit new places. Wherever they are, that is where their attention is until the picture changes. And, because these children are so social, they have no difficulty meeting new friends on their journeys.

ESFPs are impulsive and usually need to learn moderation. They do not think of future consequences and thus must learn, over time, through their experiences. As children, ESFPs have difficulty waiting. Their needs are immediate, and they become impatient when forced to put off something until a future date or a future time—and this includes waiting for a bath, another sibling, or dinner.

Fun-loving, busy, enthusiastic, witty, and warm children, ESFPs are often adored by their teachers for their willingness to try new subjects and participate in group activities. If ESFPs have a good rapport with a teacher, their love of the subject taught and school in general will increase significantly.

Activities That Encourage an ESFP's Natural Strengths: Art (drawing, painting, collage, sand art, jewelry making, and ceramics). ESFPs also enjoy the performing arts, using their bodies and a wide variety of facial expressions to entertain others and make them laugh, as well as music, collecting fine things, singing and dancing, traveling, meeting new people, and going to animal farms where the animals are well cared for (otherwise an ESFP will be very disturbed by the cruelty and neglect and will want to do something about it—now!).

What Energizes an EsFP? Meeting new people; group activities (dancing, square dancing, playing music, fun sports games, etc.); being close to others, especially those they love; having fun in a relaxed and jovial atmosphere; making others laugh and smile; creating fashion; looking for the best things in life.

What Drains an EsFP? Prolonging the attainment of goods or services, including those provided by parents; being isolated; waiting for inordinate amounts of time; austerity and iron-fisted frugality; being pushed away physically and emotionally.

What Relaxes an EsFP? Cuddling, snuggling, hugs, touch, being with a tight-knit family, hanging out with animals, creating with very detail-oriented art forms, soothing music, and being sung to by their parents.

ISFP *Personality Type*

ISFPs are very gentle and sensitive children who tend to be in the here and now. On the outside, they appear to be modest and unassuming individuals, yet they possess intense feelings that are most often expressed through an artistic medium, especially the fine arts and performing arts. Although seemingly self-contained considering their mild exterior, ISFPs need a great deal of love and affection from those close to them. They also require constant reassurance and encouragement, which can, at times, really try a parent's patience.

ISFPs are often described as "spontaneous," "inquisitive," and "free spirits." They move to their own internal rhythms and do not enjoy being rushed or bullied. If they become upset, they will usually need some quiet time or privacy to collect themselves before they can rejoin the family or a group.

ISFPs can be very expressive, yet they rarely show their more-exuberant and boisterous side to others. If they are frightened or unsure, however, ISFPs will often cry loudly with huge tears and great dramatics or withdraw. During these moments it is important to remember how much an ISFP needs to feel loved. To withhold affection and love from this child is devastating. Unlike many introverts, ISFPs are usually good at going with the flow. They enjoy new adventures: travel, car rides, being taken to an amusement park, or going to the circus. Generally, ISFPs approach new things with open arms and tend to regard whatever they encounter without judgment.

ISFPs love animals. They also love to collect stuffed animals and seem to have an eye for quality. Other children may drag home sticks and nuts and bolts found on the ground, but ISFPs prefer glass figurines, music boxes, shells, china tea cups, and the like. It makes sense that an ISFP would gravitate to the arts. They are adept at blending colors and creating designs that match in color and proportion. ISFPs do best with warm, caring teachers with whom they can develop a personal relationship and from whom they can receive one-on-one time. Praise from others goes a long way with an ISFP as they seem to need and want the validation and encouragement of others. Hurtful words can wound an ISFP and, as introverts, they may have trouble sharing their feelings, which can take a physical toll on them, especially when it takes them awhile to get over it.

ISFPs can have great concentration, which is a wonderful trait. However, they may have difficulty keeping track of time. For ISFPs the time is now. They do not usually concern themselves with the future or future events. By the same token, ISFPs don't tend to gravitate toward the abstract. It is too nebulous. Rather, they prefer to be more literal in their approach, wanting to see real results.

Activities That Encourage an ISFP's Natural Strengths: Collecting, hands-on science kits, art (drawing, painting, ceramics, and the like), yoga, tai chi chuan (both of these provide being deep within the body and focused movement), working at the zoo or a pet store as a volunteer, listening to music tapes, singing with those close to them, learning new songs by being sung to, going to the ballet and modern dance shows, and figure skating.

What Energizes an ISFP? Time alone, watching the performing arts, being deeply engaged in an art project, snuggling with those they love, making music, and feeling safe enough to be boisterous and more humorous (usually at home with family).

What Drains an ISFP? Sharp criticism, aggressive behavior (especially when it is directed toward them), feeling unloved and unappreciated, not having time to process their feelings, receiving a harsh response to their intense and often dramatic emotional expression, not getting private time.

What Relaxes an ISFP? Receiving lots of love and affection, feeling safe and secure, having a private sanctuary, head rubs, massage, soothing music, and feeling emptied out of uncomfortable feelings.

Now that you have read a detailed description of each personality type, see if your original guess still stands. I hope you have gained deeper insight into your child's temperament, as well as your own, so you can make wise choices when it comes to structured activities, methods for relaxing, and infusing the simple pleasures into your family's life.

Resources

Please Understand Me, by David Keirsey and Marilyn Bates. Del Mar, Calif.: Prometheus Nemesis, 1978.

Nurture by Nature, by Paul D. Tieger and Barbara Barron-Tieger. New York: Little Brown & Company, 1997.

Do What You Are: Discover the Perfect Career for You Through the Secrets of Personality, by Paul D. Tieger and Barbara Barron-Tieger, Boston: Little Brown & Company, 1995.

Loving Each One Best: A Caring and Practical Approach to Raising Siblings, by Nancy Samalin. New York: Bantam Books, 1996.

Organizations

Communication Consultants
20 Beverly Road
West Hartford, CT 06119
(800) YOUR-TYP (968-7897)
(860) 232-1321 (fax)

Communication Consultants provides training for professionals based on the books *Nurture by Nature* and *Do What You Are* (as listed under "Resources"). The training courses are also open to the public.

Center for Applications of Psychological Type (CAPT)
2720 N.W. 6th Street
Gainsville, FL 32609
(800) 777-CAPT
CAPT offers training programs for professionals, consulting services, and publishes type-related books and materials. CAPT also provides computer scoring of the Myers-Briggs Type Indicator and maintains the Isabel Briggs–Myers Memorial Library.

Workshop Way
P.O. Box 850170
New Orleans, LA 70185-0170
(504) 486-4871
Workshop Way is a progressive educational system based on human growth. It is located on the campus of Xavier University and offers consulting and training programs for educators who are interested in applying its methods to teaching and designing entire school system curriculums.

APPENDIX 2

Other Systems for Understanding Temperament

It is my hope that the following systems will assist you in piecing together vital aspects of your child's essence so you can apply that knowledge to the daily decisions you make on his behalf: choosing schools and baby-sitters; structuring unhurried time; pursuing enjoyed activities, alone time, and social and play time; limiting TV, bringing balance into his busy and sometimes overscheduled life; listening to his needs and wants; and, most importantly, remembering that no matter how advanced your child is, how sophisticated, how commanding of the written or verbal word, how socially or physically adept, he is still a child who needs your love, protection, and care.

The Enneagram

The Enneagram originated in the Middle East. Today, many people use it for education, psychology, and personal growth. It is a system of nine numbers, each representing a personality type. Although it is believed that each of us possesses all of the numbers or qualities inherent in each type, one number or type is the primary mode by which we operate. Below I will give a brief description of numbers one through nine and the correlating definitions of each personality. A note of caution: it is important to remember that the Enneagram, like other systems of personality and temperament, does not fully capture the qualities and depth of every individual. Rarely do any of us fit squarely into a particular category. Like all psychological systems, use it as a tool to better understand your child and the multitude of qualities he or she possesses.

The One: The Perfectionist

The Perfectionist is exactly what the name implies: one who strives for perfection. They tend to be very critical of themselves and others, always looking for a better way to improve upon things/people/ideas. Ones tend to be serious and hardworking. They like their rooms to be neat and tidy, and they can feel frustrated and agitated if they have to be in chaos or a nonorderly environment. If something is not done to their satisfaction, they will usually let you know about it, often taking a know-it-all approach. Ones can be judgmental and unbending in their ideas about how things should be. Yet, if things are done their way, Ones tend to feel happy that the other person finally "got it right." Wanting the world to be at its best, Ones tend to worry, and they try to hide their anxiety, which can become anger just below the surface. At their best, Ones are logical, analytical, balanced, and fair. And, when they relax and have fun, they can be enjoyable, creative people to know. Because Ones tend to follow the rules and, in fact, make the rules theirs, they can become overly serious and self-competitive. It is helpful for parents to encourage One children to engage in relaxing, noncompetitive, non-goal-oriented activities at least once a day. Ones also need to learn how to be more flexible in their opinions. Certainly, if they feel strongly about an issue, they can hold their position; yet it is good for them to learn how to put themselves in another's shoes from time to time. Because Ones often take on responsibilities around the house simply because they are oriented that way, it is important for parents not to overload them. Otherwise, Ones can resort to typical perfectionist behavior, feeling overburdened by responsibilities and fearing something is wrong with them because they feel this way.

The Two: The Helper

Twos gain a great deal of their sense of self through helping others. They are genuinely concerned about the needs of others and wish to assist whenever they can. They have an uncanny ability to anticipate the needs and desires of others, often placing those needs above their own. Unlike Ones, Twos openly exhibit sensitivity, and their feelings are easily hurt. A harsh word or unkind behavior can be devastating to a Two. Twos are protective of those they love and are very loyal. When they experience conflict in a relationship, especially a close friendship or family tie, they can feel betrayed and rejected. It is important that Twos learn not to take others' behaviors so personally. "You did not cause another's behavior," is a phrase parents of Twos often echo to their children. Because Twos receive so much of their validation from others, it is helpful to direct them toward their own creative pursuits, helping them to develop their own interests, especially those that are not contingent upon another's approval. Twos also need time away from other people so they can extricate themselves from the needs and wants of others and, instead, focus on their own thoughts and feelings for a change.

Twos need assistance from their parents when it comes to being "too nice." For example, a Two might offer a favorite toy to a friend as a way to gain love and acceptance, only to find that he or she ignored the consequences: "I want my toy back!" Giving is often too automatic for Twos, and they must learn that although their generous natures are admirable, they must be careful not to be taken advantage of, nor to offer things they will later regret having parted with. Twos also need assistance from their parents when they begin to use their nice behavior to manipulate others to get what they want. Helping Twos to be assertive and direct without being overbearing is essential. Because Twos are deeply emotional, parents need to be patient with Twos' feelings and expression of feelings. If Twos don't feel that their highly emotional natures are accepted, they usually feel completely rejected as a person.

Again, because Twos are so externally referented—gaining their identity from others—learning to develop their own individuality and personal preferences is vital to a balanced sense of self.

The Three: The Achiever

The Achiever also gains his or her identity from others, but it is not so much through acts of kindness as it is from concrete achievements. Threes like to be recognized for their accomplishments, whether at home or at school. They work hard to reach their goals, and their interests and abilities are varied. Threes tend to be efficient and quick-minded children who like to get things done.

They are often outgoing and have little difficulty relating to others. In fact, many Threes are extremely social people, and their natural confidence attracts others to them easily. And, because of the confidence they exude, others will follow their lead and look to Threes for direction. They see opportunity everywhere and are not afraid of challenges. Like the perfectionist, Threes place great importance on looking just right, being in style, and having a perfect image. Because they have high standards, they usually need to learn to relax more often—and not think of relaxing as being lazy and nonproductive. Threes can overwork themselves, and because they have so many goals, they can take on too much only to find that they feel scattered and overwhelmed (and stressed!). Parents of Threes need to teach Three children how to narrow their goals and focus with a step-by-step approach. Learning not to hurry and that it isn't necessary to meet every goal instantaneously is an important lesson for Threes.

Another important lesson for Threes is to become aware of their own thoughts and feelings and what pleases them. Like Twos, they often forget to check in with themselves to see if a project is enjoyable to them. Threes have lots of energy and seem to be always on the go. Parents need to ensure that plenty of repetitive, engaging, yet noncompetitive activities are available to these children. Having a pleasurable focus without a goal, having an interactive activity without having to produce, and having a calming activity that lights up Threes' senses are great ways to create greater balance in their busy, active lives.

The Four: The Romantic

Fours are notorious for being creative and dramatic individuals. They have an innate sense of the dramatic, both comic and tragic. As a result, they often find daily life to be less than ideal. In fact, to Fours, the operations and details involved in daily life can be boring and tedious. Fours prefer the movies and the arts, as they find fantasy and the endless imagination to be more engaging. Routine can be dull to Fours, and they will often seek out more adventurous activities and outlets for their creative energy. Fours enjoy mystery and twists of fate. They like to turn the ordinary into the extraordinary.

Although Fours are friendly and social, they may feel "different" and experience themselves as being outside the norm. This can create a sense of loneliness and melancholy. Fours experience their emotions strongly and can be overpowered by them at times. They have keen, perceptive natures and often notice things others do not. When they discuss their vision with others, they discover how much they actually absorb and see how fanciful their inner vision can be. It is important for parents of Fours to encourage their children's cleverness and ability to see beyond the obvious because it builds confidence and lessens the feelings of not belonging. It is also important for parents to assist Fours in respecting their feelings, then moving beyond them so as not to result in too many downward spirals of depression and unconsolable tears. Because Fours tend to feel shame when someone is angry with them, parents must take time to explain and communicate with a Four so they do not always feel as though they are to blame simply because someone is expressing uncomfortable emotions. As Elizabeth Wagele points out in her book, *The Enneagram of Parenting: The Nine Types and How to Raise Them Successfully*, "Emotional reactions can interfere with Fourish (and all children's) eating and sleeping . . . It is important for these children to feel calm and secure concerning sleeping and eating. Swallowing becomes difficult if family tension is served along with the food. Explain family situations in such a way that children realize the problems are not their fault."

Teach Fours to trust their gut responses, as they can have incredible accuracy. It will also encourage them to develop a strong sense of who they are as separate from friends or parents. A deep sense of self-worth coupled with the ability to express emotions and creativity bring greater balance— and joy—to a Four.

The Five: The Observer

Fives are the curious philosophers of life. They enjoy asking questions and probing the universe to find out how things work. They enjoy private time and don't appreciate it when others interrupt them or try to push them into activities, especially those activities they are not interested in. Often reflecting an introverted quality, Fives do not like to be put on the spot or forced to perform. They are also shy and often become nervous in front of others. Not outwardly social, Fives tend to keep to themselves, preferring to be engaged in their thoughts, their theories, and their mind's meanderings. One-on-one interaction is usually better for a Five's sensitive and shy nature. Because Fives don't like to be put on the spot, try introducing them to situations and new experiences before the actual event is to take place. If, for instance, a Five is beginning a new class (astronomy, perhaps!) take her to meet the instructor and to visit the planetarium before the first day. This will ensure greater comfort and success for a Five. In fact, the more often a parent can engage a Five in activities she truly takes interest in, the better it will be for two reasons: (1) a Five will meet other like-minded Fives, and (2) she will be able to pursue areas of study or research that may not fit into the mainstream offerings. Acceptance of Fives' need to engage their minds gives them confidence and trust in their own abilities and temperament.

Parents of Fives would do well to provide a calm, secure atmosphere for their children, as Fives tend to have very sensitive nervous systems and are prone to worrying, phobias, and fretting. Fives also do better when not surrounded by dominating people who expect them to think on their feet. Although Fives are bright, introspective people, their thoughts do not leap to their tongues as quickly and easily as other types, and this can cause them anxiety. If you are parenting a Five, try to give him as much time as he needs to reach a decision or express a thought or opinion. He will appreciate your patience and feel genuinely supported and safe. Unlike Ones and Threes, Fives do not tend to announce their accomplishments. Rather, they feel more loved and accepted if others take notice and join in their world. Asking Fives questions about the type of music, art, scientists, movies, and writers they like helps them to invite others in and makes them feel more appreciated and respected for who they are. It is essential that parents of Fives communicate honest love for and appreciation of the Observers' observations and interpretations. Not only will this create a greater sense of belonging for a Five, but it will help a Five to see his place in the world.

The Six: The Questioner

Six children question just about everything, and, because they do, they seldom feel as though they are walking on solid ground. In fact, their constant questioning can lead them to feel unsure, and so they never come up with answers to their questions, which perpetuates this cycle.

Sixes may panic over the slightest cause and be overly attentive to danger. This often translates into a need to take extra
precautions, especially where safety is concerned. On the
other hand, some Sixes exhibit courageous, quick-tempered,
and strong behavior to cover up any inner uncertainty.

Sixes like as little change as possible, and they tend not
to like surprises. Yet if their behavior takes a decided turn in
one direction or the other, they tend to overlook it. They
like to feel in control, and they want to know who to
attribute authority to. Parents can assist their Sixes by helping them build on their successes. Soon they will realize that
not all the things that could go wrong, do. And they will
have greater confidence in their abilities to choose.

Sixes are prone to anxiety and need to have plenty of
time to allay their concerns before bed and first thing in the
morning. Otherwise, they will brood over whatever is on
their minds. Help them to find ways to relax: baths, mas-
sages, head rubs, reading together (a story with no scary
monsters), and so forth.

Like spirited children (for a full description of the spirited child go to the next section), Sixes are prone to fits of
rage that may be frightening to other people. It is important
to allow Sixes to calm down and complete the cycle without an angry reaction from their parents. Conversely, Sixes
can be charming, entertaining, and sweet. And, at times,
they may use these qualities to control others in their need
to feel secure. It is best for parents of Sixes to remain balanced and centered in the midst of their children's mood
swings and fluctuating behavior. This will signal to Sixes
that they are safe and secure and their parents are with them
emotionally. Introducing Sixes to new situations gradually
can build self-esteem and make them less pessimistic about

the future. To create balance in the lives of Sixes, it is essential for parents to be patient and respectful of Sixes' worries while continuing to foster faith in the future and in themselves through concrete successes. They will feel less anxious of the unknown.

The Seven: The Adventurer

As the name implies, Sevens are risk takers extraordinaire who love to play and have fun. Seldom are these children glum. They seek out excitement and are curious about a variety of topics and experiences. Although they enjoy learning, they are not particularly well-suited to the passive input of information. And, for this reason, they usually do better with a teacher who gives them hands-on educational experiences.

Sevens have sunny dispositions and love what the world has to offer. They like to get their way, and they don't like it when others try to control them or thwart them from actively pursuing their interests. Sevens are persistent and energetic, much like spirited children, and they tend to be idealistic, involving themselves in many activities for the sheer joy of it. As parents, it is important not to underestimate the number of talents and breadth of knowledge Sevens can accumulate through their varied pursuits. Because Sevens like to sample many things, they may not stick with one thing for long. This tendency can transfer to schoolwork. It is common for Sevens to rush through assignments, not always being careful about specifics. However, be assured that if you give them your trust, eventually, things will come together for them. Just don't force it.

Sevens can be charming and funny individuals with a clever wit. At times they may use their charm to get out of trouble. But, generally, it is a reflection of their outgoing personality. When Seven children get into mischief, it is helpful for parents to let them know the rules; and gently, but firmly, prevent them from distracting you with jokes as a way of dismissing your words. Sevens thrive on freedom, and although they like to feel close to adults, they do not enjoy being restricted. Sometimes it seems that a relationship may need to be on their terms. Giving ample and positive direction for their incredible energy is usually better than giving them verbal warnings. And engaging them in something new and different is even better. Allow them to be the stars whenever possible so they will feel supported. Sevens love to feel a part of a group, a game, a party, and so forth. Like Fours, Sevens find daily routines somewhat dull. They prefer to be spontaneous and original. Trust Sevens' natural confidence, exuberant curiosity, and love of adventure instead of judging or trying to rein them in, and they will flourish. Reading to them—exciting stories, of course—and spending time winding down together at the end of a busy day will give them balance.

The Eight: The Asserter

Eights have a strong tendency toward blatant behavior, whether it is enthusiasm, anger, or standing up for themselves and others. They often give others a hard time, including teachers and other authority figures. When dissatisfied or irritated, Eights express their feelings without reservation. By the same token, they will take charge of a situation, bulldozing others to get what they want. Because Eights are so intense, it is helpful for parents to remind them, "When you bulldoze me, it is sometimes difficult for me to hear you." This can soften Eights and make them more aware of their impact on those around them. Eights need intensity and fun. They thrive out in nature, especially when met with challenges. If they fail to feel connected externally to the energy they feel internally, they may feel hurt and bereft. When they push on something, Eights want to feel it pushing back. As might be expected, they love heroic tales and breathtaking adventures.

Eights like to take control of a situation and can intimidate more-sensitive children. They can also be guilty of pushing their parents around. Again, instead of being cowed by Eights, it is best to push back. Not in terms of a power struggle, but by holding authority in a centered fashion. And, because Eights can shift blame and refuse to take responsibility for their behavior, it is important for parents to be straightforward and honest. This will gain an Eight's respect, and his or her more-vulnerable and warm side will be revealed. Although Eights can be thoughtful friends, they are not usually flexible when it comes to making plans because they tend to have their own agenda. If they become overly aggressive, let them know they are heard, then work on a compromise (or let them know exactly what you expect of them in the situation).

Because Eights are prone to angry outbursts, it is best that parents don't overreact or judge Eights harshly. Demonstrating patience and redirecting their focus are much more effective. Because of Eights' intense feelings and approach to the world, they must have time every day to relax and unwind. Reading exciting stories, playing in the bath, listening to soothing music, or being told a story with many twists and turns can all assist Eights in balancing out their internal stress.

The Nine: The Peacemaker

As the name implies, Nine children like peace and harmony. Conflict upsets them, although at times they can be very stubborn instead of merely just going with the flow. They love to snuggle and cuddle and sit on their parents' laps. They are sensitive and get their feelings hurt easily.

They can be slow to make up their minds, and they like to be accommodating of others' opinions and beliefs. Nines tend to lend a sympathetic ear. However, if something is bothering them, they may deny it, pretending that everything is fine. Occasionally, anger will seep out of these otherwise easy-to-get-along-with children, but it doesn't last long. Nines take solice in nature. In fact, they often have a deep connection and respect for the earth.

Nines tend to get along well with just about everybody, and to achieve harmony they make take on some of the traits of whomever they are with, which makes them good company. Nines tend to be easygoing and are thought of as gentle children with good hearts. Yet Nines may need assistance from parents to assert their needs and wants. If there are too many options (an overwhelming experience for Nines), parents must try to be patient until Nines can sort out their choices.

Nines enjoy a variety of hobbies, computer games, and simply hanging around the house. They are usually adaptable, but when they decide on something, their choice is firm. Unlike other types, they are rarely judgmental and aggressive. In fact, they can possess a quiet strength that friends and family will want to gravitate toward. Assisting Nines with focusing, asserting needs, and receiving genuinely felt appreciation will help to balance out their otherwise gentle and unassuming natures.

Take a look at the nine different types. Are there any that stand out? Are there aspects of several numbers that seem to fit your children? The Enneagram system includes *wings*: aspects of other numbers that are contained within the dominant number profile. For example, a One with a Two wing can be very insecure (the insecurity stemming from the influence of the Two). To explore this system more thoroughly, look to "Resources" at the end of the chapter.

The Spirited Child

Spirited children have commonly been called "difficult" or "challenging" children. Fortunately, in 1991 Mary Sheedy Kurcinka published *Raising Your Spirited Child*. Not only was she successful in illuminating the little-understood temperament of spirited children, but her work gave parents better tools for bringing out the best in them. I highly recommend Kurcinka's book for all parents, as it takes a very positive approach to raising children and respecting their innate temperaments.

Kurcinka desribes a spirited child this way: "The word that distinguishes spirited children from other children is *more*. They are normal children who are more intense, persistent, sensitive, perceptive and uncomfortable with change than other children." She continues: "When we choose to see our children as spirited, we give them and ourselves hope. It pulls our focus to their strengths rather than their weaknesses, not as another label but as a tool for understanding." Being the mother of a spirited child, and having been one myself, I can tell you that spirited children are a handful, yet they are also amazing and awe inspiring. They can be highly emotional on both ends of the spectrum, and when they set their minds to something it is like trying to pry a barnacle from a shell to get them to switch their focus. Granted, it would be easy to think of them as stubborn or difficult. Yet, as Kurcinka points out, they are simply persistent. Although this trait is not always easy for parents to contend with, it can serve children well—all the way into adulthood. The same is true of the other aspects of their temperament; their intensity, energetic style, sensitive nature, perceptive abilities, and difficulty with change.

Intensity

Spirited children experience their emotions in an intense and heightened way. They tend to play loudly; they have full and noticeable laughs. Even introverted spirited children exhibit an intensity. However, theirs is most likely to be turned inward. They can be reactive and explosive. They can exude tremendous joy and, as Kurcinka points out, "their tantrums are raw and enduring." For many parents, the volatility of a spirited child's emotions can be overwhelming and even frightening: "To ignore your child's tantrums is ridiculous. He can rage for an hour because you opened the door when he was expecting to do it himself. Send him to his room for a 'time out' and he is liable to tear it apart."

It is helpful for parents to know that spirited children cannot help their intensity. In fact, their physiology is actually different than other children's, thus accounting for the marked difference in their responses. For spirited children, a higher level of adrenalin flows through their veins, their hearts race more easily, and they feel whatever emotion or sensation in a deeper and more palpable way than others. Spirited children's nervous systems are extremely sensitive. The amount of adrenalin produced in everyday situations is higher in spirited children as normal changes, transitions, and surprises are perceived as more closely resembling fight or flight response in others. I know this from experience (my own blood tests and watching my son), and Mary Kurcinka verifed this in one of her presentations.

Knowing this, it is easier to learn not to take their behavior personally. Instead, as a parent, focus your attention on helping them to direct their energy in positive ways and teaching them more-constructive methods of impulse control, such as counting to ten or taking five deep breaths to gain perspective. Remember, a spirited child's range can take him high enough to dance with the gods and low enough to become destructive. Channeling this level of intensity is the key.

Persistence

Spirited children do not like to be rushed or hurried. Not only are they averse to change, especially quick changes without advance warning, but they are often intensely focused on something they are interested in—watching a favorite TV show, building a fort in the living room, digging holes in the backyard to trap a tiger—and stopping is difficult for them. Instead of thinking of them as uncooperative, think how you feel when you are constantly interrupted during an important phone call or while reading the paper or trying to prepare a meal. It is no different for them. Gently making eye contact and giving them plenty of time to prepare for the upcoming shift in their schedule goes a long way to smoothing out the transition from one activity to the next. It gives a spirited child time to disengage and refocus her attention.

Sensitivity

Spirited children are amazingly sensitive to sounds, scents, noises, moods, feelings, lights, textures, and tastes. As a result, they can become overwhelmed by the bombardment of external stimuli. It is not difficult to tell when a spirited child has reached his limit. There are copious tears, fits of rage, and tantrums. They will resist underwear that feels uncomfortable, tearing at the fabric; they will announce their discontent in shopping malls; and they will refuse to eat food that smells strange to them. As much as possible, respect their preferences as well as their limits. If you've gone from the noisy playground to a crowded store, you're probably crossing their threshold for stimulation. Make sure they have a good balance of activity and quiet, more relaxed hanging-around-the-house time. Again, parents may have to deal with the inconvenience of rearranging and tailoring their schedules to their spirited child's needs, but it will make the day go much better for all of you.

The clear advantage to spirited children's sensitivities is that they have an uncanny ability to notice unusual details— minute designs on flowers, a subtle scent coming from the garden, how you are feeling before even you are aware of it—and this quality can serve them throughout life in a variety of ways. They are in touch with the poetic side of life as well as possible warning signals others may not be aware of.

Perceptiveness

Because spirited children are so aware, they can get distracted by the many things that catch their eye. They notice every detail (a great quality to have if you're a writer!). On the other hand, if you're a parent trying to get your spirited child ready for school, it's another matter entirely. Your child can forget about putting on his shoes as he passes a butterfly in the window; he can have trouble concentrating on his homework because he hears neighbors playing outside; he can forget your instructions to retrieve his baseball mitt as he climbs the stairs only to spy an action figure's arm buried beneath the laundry basket. Try to be patient. Do not accuse your child of not listening. Simply remind him of the task at hand and help him to focus on your words.

Adaptability

Transitions are essential for spirited children. Because changes are not easy for them, limit the number of transitions they make on a daily basis, if possible. Let them know what the routine is, and make them aware of any alterations in the schedule ahead of time. When they're expecting sushi for dinner and all you have is pizza, it is helpful to let them know that if you could, you would supply them with all the sushi they could stomach; but you don't have it, so tonight pizza will have to do. Give them a chance to adjust while letting them know you understand their disappointment. Most importantly, strive to work *with* your spirited children, not against them. You will spend more time enjoying their abundant gifts and less time trying to change them into people they're not. In a December 1989 article featured in *Parents* magazine, therapist Julius Segal writes, "To reject kids' distinctive natures is to deny one of the central facts of human development: the extraordinary range of individual differences that characterize children from the moment of their birth."

I have only touched on the main points concerning spirited children. They are complex, highly emotional individuals who tend to have clever, creative, and boisterous souls. If you suspect that your child is spirited—they constitute 10 percent to 15 percent of the population—I highly recommend the books listed at the end of the chapter. They will guide you by providing concrete methods to create successes and build confidence and self-love in your spirited child—with the emphasis on respecting your child's innate temperament.

The Highly Sensitive Person

Highly sensitive people (HSP), like spirited ones, are in the minority, comprising only 10 percent to 15 percent of the general population. As the name clearly states, these individuals are highly sensitive in a variety of ways. They usually have an acute awareness of their environment and others' moods and are affected by both. Too much loud noise and other sensory stimulation can cause a sensitive person to withdraw and become irritable. They can easily feel overwhelmed and bombarded and, consequently, may need to retreat for quiet and stillness or cry as a release. HSP tend to be very sensitive to pain, physically and emotionally, as well as stimulants such as caffeine. HSP have an incredible depth of emotion and are moved by the arts and music. They have an ability to feel things at a level that many may not ever experience and are well able to put themselves in someone else's shoes. HSP tend to be compassionate, understanding, and conscientious. However, as Elaine N. Aron points out in her groundbreaking book *The Highly Sensitive Person: How to Thrive When the World Overwhelms You:* "When overaroused . . . a frequent state for HSP, we are anything but understanding or sensitive. Instead, we are overwhelmed, frazzled, and need to be alone."

HSP can be startled easily because, although they are extremely aware of their environment, they have a rich and engaging inner life that can occupy their focus. Just as spirited children are often accused of not listening because of their intense level of concentration, HSP can become preoccupied with whatever is going on inside of them and tune out certain things that are happening around them. Yet, because HSP take in external stimulation through their bodies, they can still feel fatigued after interactions with their environment regardless of the fact that their attention has been focused inward. As one might expect, HSP do not like when others try to get them to handle too many things at once, especially in a short period of time. Pressure is uncomfortable to HSP and often exhausting. Because of their high sensitivity, HSP respond well to aromatherapy, compassionate counselors, and body-centered therapies (of the soothing and noninvasive variety) as effective ways to relax and get rid of stress and overarousal. Because we live in a society that views sensitivity, especially, high sensitivity, as a fault, it can be difficult for HSP to feel appreciated and learn to use their gifts. Instead of respecting their traits and devising a lifestyle that accommodates them, most HSP push themselves in an attempt to feel more "normal." Most HSP have compensated over the years, trying to appear tougher, more resilient, and less affected by the outside world than they actually are. Fortunately, therapists, educators, parents, and others are becoming more aware of individuals who are highly sensitive and are making the necessary adjustments so HSP can flourish and come to more fully celebrate their temperament.

Hsp tend to process information more carefully and more extensively than most, sorting things into finer distinctions. This brain function coupled with a highly sensitive nervous system make HSP very intuitive. As Aron writes,

"HSP tend to be visionaries, highly intuitive artists, or inventors, as well as more conscientious, cautious and wise people."

It is essential for parents of sensitive children to respect and cherish the innate differences of HSP and allow for ample time for reflection, quiet, solitude, and a soothing environment. Allow time for dreaming, creating visions, practicing self-discovery, and in-depth studying of topics of interest. Don't expect your HSP to be able to handle the average person's level of stimulation. If you do, there is surely to be a meltdown. Remember, sensitive children have much to teach all of us about creating a kinder, gentler household and nation. They can help us to prioritize in order to simplify our lives and add a little more sanity amidst the chaos. At the end of this appendix I offer a variety of books to inform and assist parents who may be HSP or are raising one.

Rayid

The Rayid model for temperament and personality is one of the most complex and remarkable systems I have come across. It approaches individuals as the intricate holograms they are by describing their essences in a truly poetic and scientific way. Pioneered by Denny Johnson (a naturopathic doctor, scientific researcher of physiology, chemistry, and biology) more than twenty years ago, Rayid, like iridology, views the iris of the eye as a blueprint that can be read by studying the shape of the eye fibers along with openings and pigments in the cornea. In addition, it has identified areas of the iris that correlate with everything from physical health and constitution to intergenerational issues and personal challenges. Like the other systems, Rayid can easily identify qualities (such as introversion and extroversion, left-brain and right-brain dominance) as well as gifts and talents and areas of difficulty. The four primary structures are known as jewel, flower, shaker, and stream. The combination of iris patterns are known as shaker–jewel, shaker–flower, stream–jewel, and stream–flower. Each one is unique. Read carefully to see if you recognize your child (and, perhaps, yourself!).

Jewel

Numerous dotlike pigments in the iris indicate an intellectual, cerebral, thinking person. The dotlike pigments, which can be a variety of colors from black to yellow, are called *jewels*. From a distance small jewels are not very noticeable. Yet, up close, they appear to be speckles of color peppered throughout the cornea. These cerebral individuals direct their perceptions and feelings through internal thought and analysis. They love detail and enjoy observing. Jewels tend to be visual learners. They are usually controlled individuals, holding their emotions deep inside. Ironically, Jewels seek freedom. However, their sometimes overly analytical natures can prevent them from experiencing a sense of freedom. This is one of the challenges inherent in the Jewel persona. Jewels tend to be focused, directed, unemotional people with a highly mental disposition.

Flower

Distinctly round or curved openings in the fibers of the iris indicate an emotional type of person. *Flowers*, as the name implies, are usually gentle, soft, feeling types. They learn primarily through auditory means and, unlike the Jewels, their gestures are more animated and expressive. Flowers often "talk with their hands," and they can be playful and flirtatious individuals who move easily from topic to topic in conversation.

Flowers are typically flexible and spontaneous, and they enjoy change. They bring enthusiasm and vitality to any situation. But their ability to remain focused and endure until a project comes to completion is not always easy for a Flower. Flowers exude passion, fire, and grace, and they are quick to embrace new concepts and ideas. Often highly creative, Flowers are attracted to the arts, music, inventing, and the stage. As one might expect, Flowers can take on too much simply because they are so open and receptive to new things; yet it is essential for them to slow their pace and find stillness within to balance their interactions with the outer world. When they achieve inner peace, they can have a calming influence on those around them.

Shaker

Eyes that have jewel-like pigments and rounded openings are characteristics of *Shakers*. Shakers are highly motivated individuals who challenge the rules of convention. They not only like change, but they are compelled to create change, moving society toward higher goals. Some Shakers can become dogmatic and obsessive to the point of being dictators. When balanced, however, these action-oriented people can inspire others and create positive change.

Shakers like to move. They seek out adventure and physical exploration. They have incredible energy and can seem as though they are always in motion. Not surprisingly, Shakers communicate primarily with movement and gesture, and they prefer having a physical connection to their environment. They push themselves to the limit, which can leave them exhausted and out of balance. By learning moderation and consistency, Shakers can create change in tandem with greater stability. They need equilibrium in their dynamic lives. Often, this comes in the form of developing friendships and, eventually, partnerships with others who are more even-keeled, such as Stream individuals (whom you will learn about next).

Stream

A Stream personality is easy to detect. The fibers in their eyes are basically straight lines moving from the pupil to the edge of the iris like rays of sunshine. Unlike Shakers, whose eyes reflect their more-zealous and movement-oriented approach to life, the eyes of a Stream appear to be more placid. Stream energy is still and grounded, and those with Stream characteristics tend to be sensitive and intuitive individuals who create an aura of calm around them. Although calm, Streams are usually physical people who integrate life through the experience of their bodies. They learn visually and verbally, and a very noticeable trait is that they freely give and receive touch. In fact, their gestures can be tender and gentle and, thus, have a healing and nurturing effect on those around them. However, when blocked by stress or other imbalances, Streams can become stymied and lack an ability to assert their needs. Like HSP, Streams are incredibly sensitive to moods, emotions, and changes that take place around them. This intuitive and receptive nature can be both a blessing and a curse at times. Yet it is precisely this nature that enables Streams to be the mediators they are born to be. It is not uncommon for Streams to be massage therapists, nurses, social workers, athletes, dancers, public service officials, and health-care professionals. As Denny Johnson points out in his book *What the Eye Reveals*, "When a Stream feels he belongs, everyone around him experiences a sense of relaxation. If Streams become fearful or reactive, their attentions can become overprotective, even stifling instead of comfortably containing . . . When they are balanced in themselves, they bring a sense of integrity, stability and balance to any social situation."

Combination Structures: Shaker-Jewel

The iris structure of a Shaker-Jewel is wavy fiber lines combined with dotlike pigments strewn throughout the color of the cornea. As one might expect, Shaker-Jewels are dynamic individuals who often break new ground for others. Rarely do Shaker-Jewels take conventional routes. Instead, they prefer to be individualistic and progressive, instigating change whenever possible. They use their intellectual and analytical abilities (jewels) to be leaders in new thought and directed action. They are often superior thinkers, scientists, philosopers, and leaders; and because they are visionaries, often ahead of their time, they tend to be future oriented. Shaker-Jewels are true revolutionaries. They need to move: ideas, regimes, and the advancement of science, education, and whatever area of life they are trying to change. When balanced, they create positive change. However, they can be very demanding, cool, and aloof to those around them, their minds always fixated on a distant goal. For Shaker-Jewels, being trapped (or merely feeling that way) is their worst nightmare. They need their freedom, yet long to be understood and accepted on their terms. As a result, Shaker-Jewels are often loners who take company in their intellectual workings.

Combination Structures: Shaker-Flower

As one might imagine, the iris of a Shaker-Flower has wiry, squiggly lines in the fibers coupled with large openings between the fibers called flowers. Shaker-Flowers, like their Shaker-Jewel counterpart, enjoy creating change. Yet, because of the nurturing and sensitive influence of the Flower essence, Shaker-Flowers approach change in a less-radical and less-mental way. Dynamic communicators, demonstrative, and charismatic, they tend to inspire others with the enthusiasm of a true visionary. Naturally outgoing, Shaker-Flowers are comfortable in the public eye. Consequently, they are attracted to the media, the arts, music, politics, and economics. They also make excellent networkers who tend to look at the bigger picture. The detail-oriented follow-through of their ideas can be cumbersome and make a Shaker-Flower lose interest if a project takes an inordinate amount of time to complete. Like all Shakers, Shaker-Flowers can be extremists. They are prone to being aggressive, both physically and emotionally, yet they can just as easily be playful, entertaining, and exuberant. Mood swings are not uncommon with this type. Denny Johnson describes a Shaker-Jewel in this way, "To exist in the heart of passion and yet maintain poise is their ultimate challenge and greatest reward." When out of balance, a Shaker-Flower can be depressive and blaming. If efforts to create change in the world have been thwarted or rejected often enough, a Shaker-Flower may become cynical and despondent. On the other hand, when balanced, a Shaker-Flower can create unification, channeling enormous amounts of energy with a vital and dynamic focus.

Combination Structures: Stream-Jewel

The iris of a Stream-Jewel is a combination of fine, straight lines moving out from the center (stream) and dotlike pigments placed throughout the circumference of the cornea. Stream-Jewels are known for their ability to offer support and caring. They are a great asset to a group, offering cohesion and direction. Yet, because their style is rarely autocratic, they have a unique way of synthesizing individuals in a group, moving them toward resolution. Their insight and stability make them good healers, social workers, teachers, and managers. If they have many jewels throughout the iris, they can be very cerebral with a hunger for information. The more data they can gather, the better. Stream-Jewels have a tendency to gather and piece together information. They enjoy systems of all kinds.

Unlike the dynamic movement of the Shaker-Flower, Stream-Jewels are more methodical and less apt to change until they are sure of each step or, at the very least, the outcome. Seldom do they make hasty decisions or take big risks. Rather, their strengths lie in their nurturing, often through touch, and their ability to use information to inform and transfer knowledge to others. Often, Stream-Jewels are fond of children and freely offer what they know to others' young and growing minds. However, Stream-Jewels aren't necessarily spontaneous and playful as children. On the contrary, they can worry, be full of concern, and feel overburdened. For this reason, they often choose the more expansive and daring Shaker-Flower as a mate, instinctively creating balance between the two structures. The Stream-Jewel provides tranquility and stability while the Shaker-Flower provides movement, expansion, and serendipity. If Stream-Jewels learn to surrender—to let go of control and the need to carry others' mental burdens—they experience freedom and a deep understanding within themselves, and they are able to do what they do best: heal, nurture, and soothe.

Combination Structures: Stream-Flower

The iris of a Stream-Flower is an interesting mix of straight fibers moving from the center to the edge of the colored part of the eye (stream) and round openings between some of the fibers (flowers). Stream-Flowers tend to be very emotional individuals because of the influence of the flower structure within the eye. As one might imagine, Stream-Flowers tend to be sensitive and tenderhearted. They exude warmth, calm, and acceptance. However, they are anything but wallflowers. In fact, their athletic abilities and physical prowess are obvious, as are their social skills. Often talented athletes, performers, and healers, Stream-Flowers can be the picture of health. It is not uncommon for them to be physically beautiful as well: dancers, models, gymnasts, or beauticians. Their kind, compassionate, and nurturing natures often lead them into midwifery, natural healing, the fine arts, gardening, and work concerning animals and the care of the earth. Although they possess an earth mother quality, they are not necessarily ones to do without material possessions, wealth, power, and raw beauty. Gentle souls, Stream-Flowers have the capacity for great emotion, yet they also have more physical strength than their strictly Flower counterpart.

Stream-Flowers do not usually offer the great ideas. However, they are the ones who can carry an idea to completion, implement detailed plans, and take a concept and turn it into concrete reality. If, on the other hand, they are blocked or stressed, they can be impulsive, overly rational, neurotic, and indecisive. When balanced, they are compassionate, sensitive, emotional, and physically oriented individuals.

It is important to remember that imbalances appear in all types, as evidenced by the variety of behaviors that detract from the core essence. All Rayid types—whether Shakers, Jewels, Streams, Flowers, or a combination thereof—have inherent challenges as well as unique gifts and talents. Again, as parents, we have the opportunity to assist our child in bringing forth the best of his nature, thus diminishing the negative aspects by overcoming challenges through knowledge and wisdom. As noted earlier, the Rayid system is complex and distinct. It is an elaborate method that enables health practitioners, educators, physicians, and other professionals to "read" an individual's unique blueprint, offering insights into each aspect of that person's life with uncanny accuracy. Because it is relatively new on the scene, it is not always easy to find someone who is highly specialized in this area (but it is worth the effort). If you are interested, either for yourself or your child, I recommend you contact Rayid International to locate a practitioner in your vicinity. You also might want to order their materials to study the individual profiles in more depth. The contact information is available at the end of the appendix.

Numerology

Many systems of numerology exist. As with astrology, most people view them to be less scientific and accurate than psychiatry, psychology, and other related social sciences. Certainly, I would not recommend basing one's life strictly on numerology any more than I would any system, scientific or otherwise. Rather, use numerology as a tool, one of many, to probe the mysteries of the soul and make determinations about your identity as well as your children's. Insights are insights and they often answer questions we may not have articulated to ourselves, then point us in directions we may not have previously considered or thought possible.

Author Dan Millman offers one of the best books I've found on numerology: *The Life You Were Born to Live: A Guide to Finding Your Life Purpose*. Millman's books and tapes can be purchased from HJ Kramer, P.O. Box 1082, Tiburon, CA 94920; (800) 833-9327. The author comes from a spiritual perspective, highlighting the challenges inherent in fulfilling one's life purpose. Millman's approach is positive and straightforward with a philosophical bent.

Children are intricate and complex. Yet, in today's fast-paced world, we often diminish the rich mosaic of who they are with simplistic categories or sound-bytes that only portray a slice of their identity. This approach tends to reduce them to one-dimensional characters instead of illuminating the amazing kaleidoscope of who they truly are. But why we would want to settle for a few descriptive qualities or superficial personality profiles when we could reach further and come away with the knowledge of who our children really are? Explore. Educate yourself. Your children will be glad you did.

Resources

The Enneagram

The Enneagram of Parenting: The Nine Types and How to Raise Them Successfully, by Elizabeth Wagele. San Francisco: HarperCollins, 1997.

The Enneagram Made Easy, by Renee Baron and Elizabeth
Wagele. San Francisco: HarperCollins, 1994.

*Are You My Type, Am I Yours? Relationships Made Easy
Through the Enneagram*, by Renee Baron and Elizabeth
Wagele. San Francisco: HarperCollins, 1995.

Raising Spirited Children

Raising Your Spirited Child, by Mary Sheedy Kurcinka.
New York: HarperCollins, 1991.

The Challenging Child, by Stanley I. Greenspan. New
York: Addison-Wesley, 1995.

*The Challenging Child: A Guide for Parents of Exceptionally
Strong-Willed Children*, by Mitch Golant, Ph.D. and
Donna G. Corwin. New York: Berkeley Books, 1995.

Parenting the Strong-Willed Child, by Rex Forehand and
Nicholas Long. Chicago: Contemporary Books, 1996.

Highly Sensitive Children

*The Highly Sensitive Person: How to Thrive When the World
Overwhelms You*, by Elaine N. Aron. New York: Birch
Lane Press, 1996.

The Sensitive Child, by Janet Poland. New York: St. Martin's Press, 1995.

Rayid

What the Eye Reveals, by Denny Ray Johnson. Boulder,
Colo.: Rayid Publications, 1995.

Contact Rayid International to order educational materials,
books, and pamphlets and to sign up for conferences and
workshops:

Rayid International
P.O. Box 438
Olga, WA 98279

Todd Nelson, N.D., is highly trained in Rayid, not only for nutritional purposes but for life counseling also: (303) 744-7858 fax: (303) 202-1720 or write:
Todd Nelson, N.D.
142 West Fifth Avenue
Denver, CO 80204
tlwc@concentric.net

Numerology

The Life You Were Born to Live: A Guide to Finding Your Life Purpose, by Dan Millman. Tiburon, Calif.: HJ Kramer, 1993.

Additional Resources

The Open Mind: Unlocking the Pattern of Your Natural Intelligence for Insight, Creativity, & Better Communication, by Dawna Markova, Ph.D. Berkeley, Calif.: Conari Press, 1996.
Emotional Intelligence, by Daniel Goleman. New York: Bantam Books, 1995.
Raising an Emotionally Intelligent Child, by John Gottman. Ph.D. New York: Simon & Schuster, Fireside Book, 1997.
Teacher, by Sylvia Ashton-Warner. New York: Simon & Schuster, Touchstone Books, 1963.

Index

Active listening, 154–56
Activities
    art as important activity,
        55–60
    creativity and unrushed time,
        60–61
    encouragement of artistic
        expression, 61–66
    following your child's lead in,
        71–74
    overscheduling, 3, 8, 12, 67
    sleep as meaningful activity,
        66–68
    stress busters, 68–71
Air purification, 118
Alcoholism, 28–29
Allen, Betsy, 11
Allende, Isabel, 41
Allergies, 35–36, 113
Andersen, Nina, 111
Animals, caring for, 79, 201
Anorexia, 29–31
Antibiotics, 114–15
Anxieties and phobias, 34–35
Aron, Elaine N., 235, 236
Art
    creativity and unrushed time,
        60–61
    encouragement of artistic
        expression, 61–66
    importance of, 55–60
Attention deficit disorder and
    attention deficit
    hyperactivity disorder

defined, 23–24
and mineral deficiencies,
    111–14
resources, 24–25
Attention span, children's, 6,
    81–83
Author of this book, 256
Autistic children, 111

Ballet, 71–72
Ban Breathnach, Sarah, 42
Barron-Tieger, Barbara, 40, 46,
    192, 193
Bates, Marilyn, 46, 47, 190,
    207
Bolen, Jean Shinoda, 41, 42
Books. See also Resources
    All I Really Needed to Know I
        Learned in Kindergarten,
        73, 75
    The Argument Culture, 152,
        163
    Do Less, Achieve More, 84, 88
    Emotional Intelligence, 88, 158,
        163, 248
    The Enneagram of Parenting,
        222, 246
    Everyday Blessings, 125, 129,
        153, 160, 163
    The Everyday Work of Art, 57,
        66, 74
    Gift from the Sea, 83, 88
    The Highly Sensitive Person,
        235, 247

The Hurried Child, 2, 10, 43, 54
Kitchen Table Wisdom, 156, 163
The Life You Were Born to Live, 246, 248
Love and Awakening, 123, 129
Nurture by Nature, 40, 46, 54, 192, 215
The Optimistic Child, 131, 149
Please Understand Me, 46, 54, 190, 207, 215
Poetic Medicine, 59, 74
Raising a Family, 21, 29, 36, 149
Raising Your Spirited Child, 230, 247
Real Moments, xii, xvi
The Re-Enchantment of Everyday Life, ix, xvi, 132, 149
Relax—You May Only Have a Few Minutes Left, 166, 172
Restoring Balance to a Mother's Busy Life, 121, 129
The Road Less Traveled, 34, 36
The Seven Secrets of Successful Parents, 66, 74, 149, 163
The Shelter of Each Other, 133, 149
Simple Abundance, 42, 54
Simplify Your Life, 45, 54
20 Teachable Virtues, 137, 149
What the Eye Reveals, 241, 247
Winning the War Against Asthma and Allergies, 113
Booth, Eric, 57, 58, 66
Boredom in children, 6, 81–83
Breakfast, 104–9
Bulimia, 29–31
Bush, Barbara, 74
Busyness, xi

Camping, 92–95
Candlelighting ritual, 16–17
Carrey, Jim, 165

Chaplin, Charlie, 165, 205
Character, building, 131–49
  cooperation, 147–49
  courage, 138–39
  empathy, 137–38
  honesty, 146–47
  humor, 139–41
  optimism and virtue, 133–34
  patience, 142–44
  respect, 141–42
  self-motivation, 145–46
  self-reliance, 144–45
Chin-Ning Chu, 84
Cleaning products, natural, 117–18
Cod liver oil, 103
Communication, 151–63
  harsh words, 152–53
  importance of feelings, 157–59
  importance of listening, 154–56
  real words, 153–54
  taking time for feelings, 159–63
  true understanding, 156–57
Computer games and television
  amount of time spent on, 77–78
  and attention span, 81–83
  effects of, 80–81
  real time instead of time spent on, 83–87, 88
  time-outs from, 78–80
Cooperation, 147–49
Courage, 138–39
Cutler, Dr. Ellen, 113

Dairy products, 101
Daydreaming, 61
DeAngelis, Barbara, xii
Depression, 31–33, 131, 132
Diet. *See* Food
Discipline, 167–70. *See also* Virtues, teaching
Dyslexia and learning disabilities, 25–27

Earl of Chesterfield, 141
Eating disorders, 29–31
Ecotourism, 95
Electronic devices, 77–88
    amount of time spent with,
        77–78
    and attention span, 81–83
    and behavioral changes, 80–81
    real time instead of time spent
        with, 83–87, 88
    time-outs from, 78–80
Elium, Jeanne and Don, 21, 29
Elkind, David, 2, 3, 43
Ellovich, Dr. E. Michael, 40, 44,
    54
Emotional intelligence, 81–82,
    158
Empathy, 137–38
Enneagram system for
    understanding
    temperament, 217–30
    The Achiever, 220–21
    The Adventurer, 226–27
    The Asserter, 227–28
    The Helper, 219–20
    The Observer, 223–24
    The Peacemaker, 228–30
    The Perfectionist, 218–19
    The Questioner, 224–26
    The Romantic, 221–23
Evans, Bill, 55
Exercise, 115–17
Existential understanding, 157
Extroverts versus introverts,
    45–47

Feelings
    importance of, 157–59
    taking time for, 159–63
    thinking versus feeling types,
        47–48, 157–59
Food
    and attention deficit disorder,
        111–14
    breakfast ideas, 104–9
    lunch ideas, 109–11
    resources on, 119–20

seven rules of balanced eating,
    100–104
Fox, John, 59
Frazer, Matthew, 134
Fulghum, Robert, 73

Genoa, Dr. Estaban, 112
Goleman, Daniel, 81, 82, 158
Green Vibrance Super Food,
    103–4

Healthy living
    alternatives to antibiotics,
        114–15
    attention deficit disorder and
        nutrition, 111–14
    clean home environment,
        117–18
    exercise, 115–17
    nutritious breakfasts, 104–9
    nutritious lunches, 109–11
    resources, 118–20
    rules for balanced eating,
        100–104
Higher aims
    environments that nurture,
        135–37
    simple ways to teach
        important virtues, 137–49
Highly sensitive people (HSP),
    235–37
Hinchman, Ginger, 89
Homeopathic medicines, 114–15
Honesty, 146–47
Honig, Dr. Alice Sterling, 9
Howitt, Mary Botham, 135
Hugging and holding children, 5
Humor
    versus anger and fear, 170–71
    balancing stress with, 166–67
    benefits of, 165
    and discipline, 167–70
    as teachable virtue, 139–41

Imbalances, 17–37
    alcoholism, 28–29
    allergies, 35–36, 113

anxieties and phobias, 34–35
attention deficit disorder
    (ADD) and attention
    deficit hyperactivity
    disorder (ADHD), 23–25,
    111–14
chronic depression, 31–33
dyslexia and learning
    disabilities, 25–27
eating disorders, 29–31
post-traumatic stress
    syndrome, 20–22
Introverts versus extroverts,
    45–47

James, William, 83
Johnson, Denny, 237, 241, 242
Jong, Erica, 124

Kabat-Zinn, Myla and Jon, 125,
    153, 160
Keirsey, David, 46, 47, 190, 207
Keller, James, 129
Kurcinka, Mary Sheedy, 230,
    231, 232
Kutner, Dr. Lawrence, 8

LaRouche, Loretta, 165
Laundry disks, 117
Learning disabilities, 25–27
Leverte, Kara, x
Lewis, Richard, 56, 60
Lindbergh, Anne Morrow, 83
Listening
    importance of, 154–56
    and nature, 90–92
Lorde, Audre, 63
Lunch, 109–11

Martial arts, 73
Martin, Jeanine, xi
Marx Brothers, 165, 205
McCarthy, Judith, 96, 168
Meals
    breakfast ideas, 104–9
    lunch ideas, 109–11

seven rules of balanced eating,
    100–104
Meaningful activities
    art as important activity,
        55–60
    creativity and unrushed time,
        60–61
    encouragement of artistic
        expression, 61–66
    following your child's lead in,
        71–74
    sleep, 66–68
    stress busters, 68–71
Mentors for children
    and busy lifestyles, 121–22
    finding, 125–29
    for higher-aim growth, 136
    importance of, 122–25
Miller, Alice Duer, 155
Millman, Dan, 246
Moore, Thomas, ix, xiii, xiv, 132
Music, 55, 58
Myers-Briggs personality test,
    173–215
    abbreviations for personality
        descriptions, 174
    ENFJ personality type, 176–77
    ENFP personality type, 179–81
    ENTJ personality type, 183–85
    ENTP personality type, 187–90
    ESFJ personality type, 197–200
    ESFP personality type, 209–11
    ESTJ personality type, 192–95
    ESTP personality type, 203–6
    INFJ personality type, 177–79
    INFP personality type, 181–83
    INTJ personality type, 185–87
    INTP personality type, 190–92
    introversion and extroversion,
        45–47, 174
    intuition and sensing, 47,
        174–75
    ISFJ personality type, 200–203
    ISFP personality type, 211–14
    ISTJ personality type, 195–97
    ISTP personality type, 206–9

judging and perceiving, 48
resources and organizations
relating to, 214–15
thinking and feeling, 47–48,
175

Nambudripad Allergy
Elimination Technique
(NAET), 36, 113
Nature
for balance, 89–90
camping, 92–95
and listening, 90–92
in parks and nearby nature
centers, 96–97
seasonal activities, 96
Numerology, 245–46
Nutrition
and attention deficit disorder,
111–14
breakfast ideas, 104–9
lunch ideas, 109–11
resources, 119–20
seven rules of balanced eating,
100–104

Obesity, 99
Olarsch, Gerald, 111
Olsen, Cindy, 95
Optimism
and depression, 131–32
and virtue, 133–34
Overscheduling
dangers of, 3, 12
and erratic sleep, 67
as punishment, 8

Patience, 142–44
Peck, Dr. M. Scott, 34
Peiper, Howard, 111
Personality test, Myers-Briggs,
173–215. *See also* Systems
for understanding your
child's temperament
abbreviations for personality
descriptions, 174

ENFJ personality type, 176–77
ENFP personality type, 179–81
ENTJ personality type, 183–85
ENTP personality type, 187–90
ESFJ personality type, 197–200
ESFP personality type, 209–11
ESTJ personality type, 192–95
ESTP personality type, 203–6
INFJ personality type, 177–79
INFP personality type, 181–83
INTJ personality type, 185–87
INTP personality type, 190–92
introversion and extroversion,
45–47, 174
intuition and sensing, 47,
174–75
ISFJ personality type, 200–203
ISFP personality type, 211–14
ISTJ personality type, 195–97
ISTP personality type, 206–9
judging and perceiving, 48
resources and organizations
relating to, 214–15
thinking and feeling, 47–48,
175
Personality type profiles
lively, intellectual child, 50–52
quiet, sensitive child, 49–50
refined dramatic, 52–53
Pessimism, 131
Pets, 79, 201
Phobias, 34–35
Physical symptoms of stress, 13
Pica, 111
Pillows, healthy, 118
Pipher, Mary, 133
Poetry, 59, 63–64
Positive stress, 9, 12
Post-traumatic stress syndrome,
20–22
Prayer, 16, 161

Rayid model for understanding
temperament, 237–45
Reading Development, Institute
of, 20

Real time, 83–87
  attention, 85
  authenticity, 85–86
  books encouraging, 88
  presence, 84–85
Recipes
  breakfast, 104–9
  lunch, 109–11
Reichtman, Peggy, 123, 124
Remen, Dr. Rachel Naomi, 156,
  157
Resources
  on alcoholism, 28–29
  for allergies, 36
  for anxieties and phobias,
    34–35
  on art and other meaningful
    activities, 74–75
  for attention deficit disorder,
    24–25
  on character building, 149
  for chronic depression, 33
  on communication, 163
  for dyslexia, 27
  for eating disorders, 30–31
  on effects of technology on
    children, 87
  for healthy living, 118–20
  humor, 171–72
  on mentors, 129
  and Myers-Briggs personality
    test, 214–15
  on nourishing with nature,
    97–98
  for post-traumatic stress
    syndrome, 21–22
  on real time, 88
  on stress felt by children,
    10
  on temperament types, 54,
    246–48
Respect, 141–42
Rolfe, Randy, 66

St. James, Elaine, 45
Scrivani, Andrew, 11, 36, 68, 74

Searle, Christine, 95
Segal, Julius, 234
Self-motivation, 145–46
Self-reliance, 144–45
Seligman, Dr. Martin E. P.,
  131
Sleep, importance of, 66–68
Spirited children, 230–35
Spirituality, 15–17
Stress
  balancing stress with humor,
    166–67
  from overscheduling, 3, 8, 12,
    67
  positive, 9, 12
  seriousness of, 9–10
  signs of, 13–15
  from too little sleep, 67
  from too many fun things, 7
Stress busters, 68–71
Success, defining, 2
Sugar consumption, 100–101
Systems for understanding your
    child's temperament
  Enneagram system, 217–30
  highly sensitive people (HSP),
    235–37
  Myers-Briggs Type Indicator,
    45–48, 173–215
  numerology, 245–46
  Rayid model, 237–45
  resources on, 246–48
  spirited children, 230–35

Tactile activities, 70–71
Tannen, Deborah, 152
Television and computers
  amount of time spent with,
    77–78
  and attention span, 81–83
  effects of, 80–81
  real time instead of time spent
    with, 83–87, 88
  time-outs from, 78–80
Temperament, your child's,
  39–54

benefits of understanding,
39–41
dangers of ignoring, 42–43
importance of knowing,
41–42
and mentors for your child,
136
Myers-Briggs Type Indicator,
45–48, 173–215
nurturing individual
differences of, 43–45
systems (other then Myers-
Briggs) for
understanding, 217–48
three profiles of different
temperaments, 48–53
Thinking versus feeling types,
47–48, 157–59
Tieger, Paul D., 40, 46, 192, 193
Touch, importance of, 5
Tree of life project, 65–66

Unell, Barbara C., 137, 138, 140
Unrushed time
and creativity, 60–61

importance of, xii, 4–9
versus real time, 83–87

Virtues, teaching
cooperation, 147–49
courage, 138–39
empathy, 137–38
honesty, 146–47
humor, 139–41
and optimism, 133–34
patience, 142–44
respect, 141–42
self-motivation, 145–46
self-reliance, 144–45
Vitamin supplements, 103

Wagele, Elizabeth, 222
Walker, Alice, 41
Water, 102
Welwood, John, 123
Whyte, David, 85
Williams, Robin, 170
Wilson, Beth, 256
Wyckoff, Dr. Jerry L., 137, 138,
140

About the Author

Beth Wilson is the mother of three and the bestselling author of books for women and mothers. She believes women can create a meaningful life of those things that are most important to them. Currently, for Wilson, this means promoting her upcoming books; working on other writing projects, including three screenplays; conducting workshops around the country, primarily for mothers; contributing to the hi-tech sales team of OnDemand, Inc., a start-up computer company based in the Silicon Valley; and experiencing the joys and challenges of raising a family.

Her previous book, *Restoring Balance to a Mother's Busy Life* (NTC/Contemporary Books), inspired her workshops of the same name, giving mothers the opportunity to experience balance first-hand while raising their children. Balance is the topic she addresses most frequently, whether on TV and radio appearances or speaking to various organizations around the country.

To obtain information on her appearance schedule or to order books and register for workshops, please visit her website at www.bethwilsonbooks.com. If you wish to contact her, please write to:

Beth Wilson
P.O. Box 1131
Belmont, CA 94002
(650) 654-1202

Wilson lives in Northern California with her family.